Securing PCs and Data in Libraries and Schools

A Handbook with Menuing, Anti-Virus, and Other Protective Software

Allen C. Benson

Neal-Schuman Publishers, Inc.
New York   London

Published by Neal-Schuman Publishers, Inc.
100 Varick Street
New York, NY 10013
Copyright © 1997 by Allen C. Benson

Printed and bound in the United States of America.

This book is designed to provide information about PC security. Although every effort has been made to make this book as accurate as possible, neither Neal-Schuman Publishers, Inc., nor the author can guarantee the accuracy or completeness of the information. The author and Neal-Schuman Publishers, Inc., shall have neither liability nor responsibility to any person or entity with respect to any loss or damages arising from the information contained in this book or from the use of the applications contained on the CD-ROM accompanying this book.

Library of Congress Cataloging-in-Publication Data

Benson, Allen C.
    Securing PCs and data in libraries and schools : a handbook with anti-virus, menuing, and other protective software / Allen C. Benson.
        p.   cm.
    ISBN 1–55570–321–6
    1. Computer security. 2. Microcomputers—Access control. 3. Data protection. I. Title.
QA76.9.A25B46   1998
005.8—dc21   98–9355
                                                  CIP

Table of Contents

Introduction

In Clifford Stoll's *The Cuckoo's Egg*, an unauthorized user breaks into one of the computers at Lawrence Berkeley Laboratory in the late 1980s. A 75¢ accounting error leads Stoll on an international chase. He eventually teams up with the FBI, the CIA, and the German Bundepost to track down a hacker/spy named Markus Hess.

Chances are that you will not be experiencing the intrigue and mystery of an international spy breaking into your organization, but you will be confronted with virus attacks and individuals trying to guess passwords, delete files, steal computer equipment, and gain unauthorized access to programs.

Technical professionals huddled behind UNIX systems and network servers may argue that PCs are not sophisticated enough to warrant special security considerations. The fact is that PCs share data. Many users access the same machine and share the same applications, which means that PCs do present security risks. Even the smallest organizations need to plan for some level of protection if their computers and data are shared.

As you begin developing a secure system in your organization, the goal to strive for is a balance between your organization's need to protect its computers and data and the user's need for flexibility. Offering more flexibility and greater access to user-friendly applications increases your organization's risks by opening security holes. Shackling your system with excessive regulations and passwords inhibits everyone's ability to work effectively, including staff.

This book offers an approach to securing your PCs that falls somewhere between these two extremes. *Securing PCs and Data in Libraries and Schools* provides you with the tools you need to assess your risks and then to reduce those risks to an acceptable level.

WHAT IS COVERED IN THIS BOOK?

Chapter 1 addresses fundamental management responsibilities including planning for a secure system, organizing computer-related information, assessing the risks that threaten your system, and disaster recovery.

Chapter 2 covers writing and implementing security policies and training staff. This chapter offers a sample security policy that easily can be adapted to meet most organizations' needs.

Chapter 3 delves into the secret world of hacking and explores why and how hackers hack personal computers. I explain some of the better-known attack scenarios and show you how you can counter these attacks.

Chapter 4 addresses physical security issues. In this chapter, I describe a variety of anti-theft devices for computers and peripherals including restraining devices and motion detectors.

Chapter 5 covers front-end security for MS-DOS and Windows. The simplest systems for maintaining adequate security use menus and password protection, and this chapter introduces some of the most popular and effective applications in this area.

Chapter 6 explains how to protect your system against major damage from viruses. It offers tips on which software to buy and tells you how to detect viruses, recover from virus attacks, and stay current on the latest viruses that are threatening PCs.

Chapter 7 addresses issues of privacy. Details are presented on how to encrypt and decrypt e-mail transmissions, hide data on your local hard drives, secure Word for Windows documents, shred files, and more.

Chapter 8 explores Internet-related security issues ranging from anonymous remailers and anonymizers to cookies and Java applets. Special attention is given to Netscape Navigator, showing you how to make it more secure on public-access PCs.

WHAT IS NOT COVERED IN THIS BOOK?

Network operating systems—such as Novell NetWare, Microsoft Windows NT, and UNIX—all have their own built-in security features. Still, they all present serious security problems because the potential exists for many users—some friendly and some not so friendly—to access their systems. Although LAN (Local Area Network) and WAN (Wide Area Network) security is important, discussing the technologies that go into establishing a secure network environment or UNIX box is beyond the scope of this book.

It could be argued that securing LANs begins with securing the most insecure technology on the network—personal computers. Network operating systems may provide extensive security options, but these can be weakened by individual PCs that are inherently insecure. Because a multitude of online and print resources already address LAN security, network operating systems, and the attack scenarios hackers use for breaking into UNIX-based systems, I have chosen to focus my attention on PC security. This same limit in scope applies to Chapter 3 where the subject of hacking is addressed. Here I am primarily concerned about hackers hacking personal computers.

WHAT IS ON THE CD-ROM?

On the *Securing PCs and Data in Libraries and Schools* CD-ROM, you find many of the programs referred to throughout this book along with a wealth of other utilities relating to PC security. The contents of the CD-ROM are organized under these eleven headings:

- Access control utilities
- Anti-virus
- Cryptography
- Digital signatures
- File back-up
- File shredding
- Miscellaneous
- Password management utilities
- Secure menu systems for Windows 3.x and Windows 95
- Viewing and editing in hex
- Text files

You will find instructions on how to use the CD-ROM in the Appendix. Consult the *readme.txt* file either in the Appendix or on the CD-ROM for an explanation of each directory's contents and a brief description of each application.

WHO SHOULD READ THIS BOOK?

This book is written for teachers and librarians and anyone else who uses a PC—especially anyone working in an organization that supports public-access PCs. If you personally do not use a PC, you still can use this book as a reference tool for learning more about security issues covered in the daily news, especially issues relating to Internet security such as hacking, secure online transactions, hostile Java applets, and e-mail encryption.

References to information on the Web and the applications that are used for accessing Web resources and services are made throughout this book. Those readers who want a thorough introduction to computers, telecommunications, Internet applications in general, and the Web specifically, should consult *The Neal-Schuman Complete Internet Companion for Librarians.*

CONVENTIONS

This book uses the short-cut method of writing Web addresses: *java.sun.com/sfaq/* instead of *http://java.sun.com/ sfaq*. On your own, you can further shorten any URLs you find that begin with *www.* and end with *.com*. For example, for *www.netscape.com* you can simply enter

netscape in your browser's Location: box. Other formats for displaying certain types of data include these:

- Commands are shown in **boldface** type.
- URLs and file names are shown in *italic* type.
- Terms being defined or introduced for the first time are presented in *italic* type.

Chapter 1

Managing Your Facilities and Assessing Your Risks

One of the most feared expressions in modern times is "The computer is down."
—Norman Augustine

Computer security in schools and libraries is ordinarily the province of technical specialists, especially in the larger systems. These organizations customarily employ full-time system administrators who, among other things, maintain the security of the computer facilities. In smaller organizations where there are no system administrators, the person who knows the most about computers is christened *the computer person.* At the bottom of the security food chain are the organizations that have one or two computers and no computer person. These organizations rely on students, parents, library patrons, and professional consultants to take care of things as they break.

Whatever level of computer expertise exists in your organization, and however large or small your system is, you should implement some level of security for your hardware, software, and data. In this chapter, I describe the beginning steps of that process. I start by introducing you to a filing system that helps you organize all your support manuals and floppy disks. Managing your computer-related documentation is a prerequisite to managing effectively even the smallest computer system.

Next, I explain the process of assessing your risks and help you identify which of your assets you want to protect. This must be done before you begin drafting a policy statement, which is covered in Chapter 2. Another concern I address in this chapter is disaster recovery—what to do when something goes wrong. This discussion covers backing up data, installing backup power supplies and surge suppressors, and making emergency startup disks.

KEEPING TRACK OF MANUALS AND DISKS

Before you try to implement a security plan, you should first implement a system for organizing all the paperwork, floppy disks, security keys, and passwords associated with your system. If you have only one PC in your building, you probably aren't having many problems keeping track of the original software, software manuals, and hardware manuals. When you add a second PC, things become more involved. Now you have to keep manuals and hardware specifications separate. You have twice as many serial numbers to track, and you cannot just say, "The PC is down" when one of the computers breaks. Now you have to specify *which* PC is down. As you add more peripherals and PCs to your system, it becomes essential that you develop a system for organizing all the computer-related information you acquire.

Four important steps will help you get started tracking your computer information. These steps are beneficial whether you are building a system from the ground up or you already have one in place:

1. Assign a name to every PC in your system.
2. Set up a database for keeping track of each PC's configuration.
3. Make a schematic drawing of your system.
4. Set up a filing system for software and hardware manuals.

Security Newsletter

Secure News at *www.isecure.com/newslet.htm* is a newsletter for data and system security, sponsored by Innovative Security Products. Their home page includes information on hardware and software security, a security FAQ, and white paper. (White papers are short essays written for educating customers.)

Why Should You Name Your PCs?

If you had only one PC in your school library, you could just call it *the computer over there*. Everyone would know which one you were talking about. When you add a second PC, you have to be more specific and say, "The PC in technical services is down," or "The hard drive on the PC upstairs just crashed." Add a second PC upstairs and you have to take a moment to describe which PC upstairs it is you are talking about. You can imagine the problems you encounter when you add 10 or 20 PCs to your system. (Administrators of large network systems inventory their networks by using network management suites such as McAfee's Zero Administration Client Suite. Details on this and other management software can be found in a sidebar later in this chapter under the heading "How Do You Perform Risk Analysis?")

Remembering names is easier than remembering numbers, so consider giving each PC in your system a name. Naming PCs serves two purposes: (1) Naming is an effective tool for linking files and database records to specific machines; and (2) When people talk about specific machines, they can call the PCs by their names rather than trying to explain where the machine is located in the building.

The first time I applied this idea, the staff and I chose a theme for naming PCs. Alexandrite, Amber, Diamond, and Zircon were named after gemstones. We ended up with 23 PCs in all and after a few months, everyone knew each PC by name. Where I'm currently working, the PCs are named Hickory, Cedar, Pine, Redbud, Dogwood, and so on—all trees indigenous to our area of the Ozarks. You can use any naming scheme you like, planets, stars, insects, cars, or even French novelists—whatever works for you. If you have more than 25 or 30 PCs in your system, you may prefer numbering them something like Telstar001, Telstar002, Telstar003, etc.

Once all your PCs are named, you can begin setting up systems for keeping track of the hardware and software. File folders or database records for a PC named Magnolia will also be labeled Magnolia, *not* the name for the PC that sits next to the coffee machine in technical services! Print a name label using 72–point typeface for each PC. Use strong, clear plastic tape to attach the label to the top of the CPU case. (Attach it so that if you need to slide the case off to work inside, the tape won't interfere.)

Creating a Database for Managing Information

Now that you've named all of your PCs, begin recording in a database important information about each PC. The advantage of storing data in digital format is that you can change it, update it, or move it around with considerable ease. These records will be valuable to you, for example, when you consider upgrading the memory in your PCs, when you need serial numbers for your insurance policy, or when a consultant asks you the storage capacity of a particular machine's hard drive.

Figure 1–1 illustrates a paper form that you can use to collect data on each PC in your system. After you have collected all of the pertinent information, enter it into a database, such as Microsoft Access or FileMaker Pro (www.claris.com/).

Building a Filing System

After you finish naming your PCs and describing their configuration, the next step is to set up a software and hardware filing system. The hardware-related file drawers contain files named after each PC in the system. This is where you store the motherboard manual, operating system manuals, modem manuals, CD-ROM drive manuals, etc. The software-related file drawers contain files named after applications; for example, MS-Office, Adobe Acrobat, PKZIP, WinU, Trumpet Winsock, Netscape, and so on.

Computer name	Diamond
Microprocessor	486DX
Serial number on case	C3452Y85
Memory	16MB RAM (Two 72–PIN 2X36 8MB)
Floppy disk A (size)	3.5–inch
Floppy disk B (size)	5.25–inch
Hard drive	1GB
CPU speed (MHz)	66
Manufacturer	DTK Computer
Serial number	129086755
Monitor (Model & Size)	AOC SVGA 17–inch
Monitor serial number	1–9897375
Location	Branch library/Branch Manager's office
Date of purchase	7/5/93
Purchase price	$1,835
Warranty	Two years from purchase
Vendor	Computing Services, Inc.
Menu items (if applicable)	1) Spreadsheet 2) Word Processor 3) Web 4) OPAC
Modem	14.4 GVC Internal Modem
Modem line number	860–6854
Network printer connections	LPT1 Laser Jet P1
Video adapter	Trident 1MB
Special notes	Boot-up password is FO03#TO; Internet service provider login userid is TRISTAR and password is CAAL9X.
Sound card	Orchid Soundwave 32
Network adapter	NE2000 PLUS

Figure 1–1: A sample computer equipment information sheet.
You can find a blank copy of this form on the CD-ROM that accompanies this book. Look in the TEXT directory for the file named DATA.DOC.

Hanging files work best for holding the wide range of materials associated with computers: floppy disks, security keys, and manuals of all sizes and shapes. If you are budgeting for equipment, figure that it takes one file drawer to hold the disks and user manuals for every four or five computers. If your file cabinets are used to store keys and passwords, make sure that the drawers have locks.

The hardware files are also an excellent place to store emergency backup materials on each PC. I make sure that each file contains an emergency boot disk (these are discussed at the end of this chapter), any pertinent passwords (screen saver passwords, CMOS passwords, passwords for exiting secure menu systems, etc.), a printout of the hard drive configuration from CMOS, and keys for locking keyboards or other security devices.

If you have batch files running on a PC that make loading anti-virus software particularly tricky, you can file installation notes for that PC in its corresponding hardware file.

A Picture Is Worth a Thousand Words

The last step in the organizational process is to create a drawing of your system. You can use an illustration program like Corel Draw, cut and paste clip art, or hire a professional to create the image. The idea is to make a visual representation of your system so that you can view all of its parts at a glance—PCs (along with their names), printers, scanners, routers, repeaters, etc. You can even show the exact length of coax cable that runs between each PC on your LAN, as illustrated in Figure 1–2.

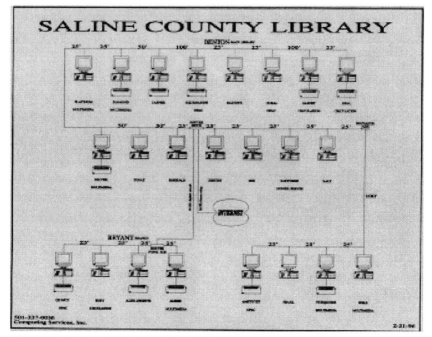

Figure 1–2: Drawing of a local area network.
(Reprinted with permission by David Jackson, Computing Services, Inc.)

What about Peripherals?

Printers and scanners and CD-ROM towers also can be named, or you can go with something simple like P1 and P2 for Printer 1 and Printer 2. Attach a label to the hardware itself, set up a hardware file to organize your printer manuals and disks with drivers, and enter pertinent data into your database records (serial number, make, model, price, date of purchase, etc.).

With a clear picture of what constitutes your system and where each item is located, it will be easier to implement your security plan. Organizing all your hardware and software also will make your work easier when it comes time to upgrade your PCs, implement disaster recovery, add new

PCs to your system, buy insurance, reload software, or find a specific manual or security key.

WHAT IS RISK ANALYSIS?

It is widely known that the proper level of security protection is determined by what you are trying to protect. For example, a PC that is 15 years old and runs only one program—a DOS-based word processor—deserves little or no investment in security protection. But a $9,000 network file server with 200,000 database records stored on its hard drive deserves your highest level of security protection.

Risk analysis is the process of looking at your entire system and deciding whether there is anything worth protecting, and if so, determining whether there is any exposure to security threats. A *security threat* is an event that potentially could compromise the integrity, privacy, or functionality of your computer system.

HOW DO YOU PERFORM RISK ANALYSIS?

Risk analysis can be performed in three steps:

1. First, take a long, hard look at your system and decide which components are at risk.
2. Next, examine how threats might manifest. Consider one machine at a time and ask yourself, "What could go wrong?"
3. The analysis concludes with recommendations on how to safeguard against threats by using various methods of protection, prevention, detection, and recovery.

Begin by Taking an Inventory

Begin your risk analysis by listing all of the computer components in your system that are subject to security threats. Drawings like the one presented in Figure 1–2 can help you inventory your equipment. Also consider which applications and data would need to be replaced if disaster struck. You may not be able to think of everything all at once, so expect this step to be an ongoing process. If your system is large, you may want to consider using an inventory system such as Zero Administration Client Suite developed by McAfee to help you keep track of everything you have.

Network Management Systems

McAfee's Zero Administration Client Suite can help you inventory the software on your network; help you keep track of your hardware including amount of memory, make and model, hardware settings, disk configurations, devices that are installed, and more; record important operating system information, such as CMOS settings, user IDs, and TCP/IP information. Zero Adminsitration Client Suite also does menuing and desktop control. To learn more, go to McAfee's Web site at *www.mcafee.com* or call 800–332–9966.

Two other network and systems management applications you might want to consider are Seagate Desktop Management Suite developed by Seagate Software Network & Systems Management Group, at *www.seagatesoftware.com*, 800–525–5645; and Norton Administrator for Networks developed by Symantec Corp., at *www.symantec.com*, 800–441–7234.

Determine How Threats Might Manifest Themselves

After you determine which components in your system are at risk, think about what could go wrong and how various threats might manifest themselves. Think about worst-case scenarios. What would you do if the hard drive on your computer crashed this afternoon? Would critical data be lost—maybe an annual budget or grant proposal, for example? How important is the data? Is it important enough to invest in a tape backup system that backs up your entire hard drive periodically, or would it suffice to copy certain critical files to a floppy disk whenever you make changes?

Another issue to consider is tape failures. What would you do if you discovered that the archival digital tapes you have been storing for the last 10 years were no longer playable? How important is the information stored on those tapes? Would you be losing local historical information? Is it valuable enough to transfer to a more durable storage medium—such as CD-ROM or optical disk—while you still can? Is it the only record in existence?

Threats may come from a number of other sources including:

- Hardware failures
- Blackouts and brownouts
- Individuals tampering with or stealing hardware, software, or data
- Extreme temperatures or humidity
- Damage from broken water pipes, spilled drinks, or fire
- Damage from floods, earthquakes, or other natural disasters
- Software failures

- Hackers
- Crackers
- Viruses
- Human error that results in bad data
- Disgruntled employees
- Disk or tape failures
- Power surges
- Interruptions in power supply

Use the PC Security Checklist shown in Figure 1–3 to help you determine potential threats to your system. Each individual computer in your system has its own special functions and unique location in the building, so perform your security analysis on a station-by-station basis.

You can find a copy of the PC Security Checklist on the CD-ROM that accompanies this book. Look in the TEXT directory for a file named *CHECK.DOC*.

Begin Assigning Safeguards

When you finish listing how each threat might manifest itself in your system, assign cost-effective safeguards. Your list should include safeguards that do the following:

- Protect hardware
- Protect software
- Protect data
- Detect viruses
- Detect attempted break-ins
- Prevent virus attacks
- Protect against power surges or blackouts
- Prevent attacks from hackers or crackers
- Deter thieves

PC Security Checklist

Computer Name:_____   Date:_____

As you consider each item in this survey, decide whether it poses a threat to your system.

- ❏ Do you have an emergency backup/rescue disk?
- ❏ Is there memory-resident anti-virus software running?
- ❏ Is the virus protection software capable of detecting macro viruses?
- ❏ Is the virus protection software updated periodically?
- ❏ Is there a password protecting CMOS setup?
- ❏ Is the bootup password set?
- ❏ Is there a secure menu system that loads at startup?
- ❏ Are the Windows 95 executables winfile.exe, taskman.exe, winhlp32.exe, control.exe, explorer.exe, and progman.exe renamed?
- ❏ Are *.ini files hidden?
- ❏ Are restrictions set in Windows 3.x progman.ini?
- ❏ Are critical data files password protected and/or hidden?
- ❏ Is the hardware secured with cables and padlocks or are other locking devices used?
- ❏ Is there a keyboard lock?
- ❏ Is the hard drive backed up?
- ❏ Are backup tapes stored off-site?
- ❏ Is the PC plugged into a surge suppressor power strip?
- ❏ Is the power strip overloaded or daisy chained?
- ❏ Are extension chords worn out or lying in walking paths?
- ❏ Are the modem and the phone line from the wall socket plugged into special ports on the surge suppressor?
- ❏ Is there a standby power system (UPS) for PCs running critical processes?
- ❏ Are sensitive data files encrypted?
- ❏ Is Java disabled in Netscape?
- ❏ Is the cookies.txt file read-only or are cookies disabled from the browser?

Figure 1–3: A security checklist to help you recognize potential threats in your computer system.
You can find a blank copy of this form on the CD-ROM that accompanies this book. Look in the TEXT directory for the file named CHECK.DOC.

- Recover damaged or lost data
- Recover virus-infected files

As you consider the risks associated with each PC, think about the time and money it takes to secure a PC and balance that against the likelihood of someone misusing or abusing it. It is impractical, for example, to spend time and money putting locks on useless files. Likewise, you are not exercising good judgment if you spend $150 on cables and padlocks to secure an older model PC with a monochrome monitor that sits in clear view of the staff during open hours.

What do you really stand to lose if your system's security is compromised? This is the question you must answer before you can determine which security tools to buy, how sophisticated they should be, and how much time and money to invest. The process of assigning safeguards is closely related to the next topic: disaster recovery.

WHAT IS DISASTER RECOVERY?

It is important for you to do your best to maintain the accuracy and integrity of the information you provide. You should also maintain systems that offer secure, safe environments in which everyone can work. When something goes wrong that jeopardizes either of these responsibilities, you need a contingency plan. Your backup plan should enable you first to respond to the crisis, and second, recover. This whole process is called *disaster recovery*.

As you read through the following sections, you see that successful recovery is dependent on taking certain preventative measures. The three most important preventative measures you can take that will help you recover from the majority of disasters are

1. Backing up data
2. Installing emergency power supply backups and surge suppressors
3. Making emergency startup disks

HOW DO YOU PREPARE FOR A DISASTER?

Disaster recovery planning should involve personnel from every department in your organization. This will encourage a broader understanding of everyone's work areas, special vocabularies, work habits, and priorities. Your contingency plan should cover what actions to take when an accident occurs. Two questions need to be answered: (1) Who will respond when disaster strikes; and (2) How will they recover?

If you already have someone on your staff who is competent in restoring lost data, removing viruses, backing up systems, etc., then that is the person who should respond in emergency situations. Make sure that you have a backup plan in place when that person leaves on vacation. If your organization is too small to have a full-time system administrator, train someone to take care of emergencies.

At a minimum, every organization should have one or more individuals who know how to backup critical data and deal with virus attacks. Hard drive crashes and computer virus attacks are two of the most common disasters from which you will have to recover. To learn more about recovering from virus attacks, have your staff read Chapter 6 and pay special attention to the section titled, "What Should You Do When You Detect a Virus?"

Protecting against System Crashes and Freeze Ups

Norton CrashGuard for Windows 95, from SYMANTEC/Peter Norton Product Group, is a crash protection and recovery program designed to help you intercept and repair many of your hung applications and system crashes. CrashGuard runs in the background and attempts to intercept crashes before your work is lost and gives you the extra time needed to save work when applications freeze up. You can download a free trial version of CrashGuard at *www.symantec.com/trialware/dlcg20.html.*

Nuts & Bolts from Helix Software is a suite of three utilities designed to protect your system from crashes and to encrypt and compress files. *Bomb Shelter* attempts to intercept a program before it crashes. This gives you a chance to save your work before it is lost. *Stronghold* enables you to encrypt files so only authorized users can access them. You can encrypt files by simply dragging them onto the Stronghold icon that sits on your desktop. *Zip Manager* is a utility that helps you compress files and create self-extracting archives. Nuts & Bolts is Freeware; however, if you purchase and register the product, you get access to several other utilities including a file shredder (these are introduced in Chapter 7), and registry wizard. You can download Nuts & Bolts from Helix Software Company at *www.helixsoftware.com/zd_downloads.html.*

Backing Up Data

Making regular backups of your critical data is important in case your hard drive crashes or data is lost due to virus attacks. Backing up may be as simple as copying one or two critical files to a single floppy disk and taking them home with you at night. For example, you may have only three critical files you're working on—a grant proposal, a journal article, and the budget. If you have a hundred hours invested in these documents, it would be worth your time to back them up to a floppy disk.

If you save your files to one of the network drives on the server, and your system administrator does an image backup daily (performs a complete backup of every file on the hard disk), it may seem redundant for you to back up important text files to a floppy disk. It's not. If the file server's hard drive crashes, there may be a period of time where your access to the server is cut off. Worse yet, there may be problems encountered restoring the server's backup tape to a new hard drive. It is also possible that the server isn't being backed up daily as you might think, so it never hurts to have that extra backup saved to a floppy disk.

Other storage devices that can be used for backing up data are shown in Table 1–1. The storage capacities of these devices range from 100MB Zip disks to 2.6 terabyte tape drives.

Buying Backup Tape Drives

There are several points to consider before investing in a tape backup system. First, make sure that when you purchase a backup tape drive, its storage capacity matches

Table 1.1: PC backup and data storage devices

Product Name	Storage Capacity	Approx. Cost	Web Source
Avatar Shark 250 external hard drive	Avatar drives use 2.5" "hardiskettes" that hold 250MB of data	External drive $300; one disk $39	www.goavatar.com/
Colorado T3000	Up to 3.2 GB capacity using 2:1 compression; 2.5 GB native	Internal drive $170; One TR-3 minicartridge $35	www.hp.com/tape/colorad o/index.html
Colorado 5 GB	Up to 5 GB capacity using 2:1 compression; 2.5 GB native	Internal $215, External $270; One 5 GB minicartridge (2.5 GB native capacity) $28	www.hp.com/tape/colorad o/index.html
Hewlett Packard SureStore CD-Writer	650MB of data, or 74 minutes of audio	External - Parallel or SCSI $580 Internal $480	hpcc997.external.hp.com/ cdwriter/main.html
Iomega Zip™ Drives	100MB Zip™ disks	$150 for an external parallel or SCSI drive; pack of 3 disks $50	www.iomega.com/product /zip/index.html
Iomega 2.0GB Ditto™ Drives	2GB maximum with compression; 1GB native	$150 for an external drive; pack of 3 disks $50	www.iomega.com/product /ditto/index.html
Iomega 1 GB Jaz™ Drive	1GB of data on a single disk	$300 for an internal; $400 for an external drive; 1 disk $124	www.iomega.com/product /jaz/index.html
MediaLogic SLA Tape Libraries (SLA - Searchable Library Architecture)	98 Gigabytes to 2.6 Terabytes	Prices start at $6,150	www.zsource.com
Microsolutions Backpack 8000T Tape Drive (plugs into your parallel port)	8GB on a single TR-4 tape	External drive $550; 3M Travan TR-4 cartridge $40	www.microsolutions.com/

MicroSolutions Backpack external 2.1GB hard drive	2.1GB hard drive	External drive $490	www.microsolutions.com/
MicroSolutions Backpack external 3.1GB hard drive	3.1GB hard drive	External drive $560	www.microsolutions.com/
Philips EasyWriter 2X/6X CD Recorder	650MB of data, or 74 minutes of audio	External $580 Internal $480	philips-support.nvcom. com/products/index.htm
Ricoh MP6200S - 2X/6X CD-Rewritable Drive	650MB of data, or 74 minutes of audio	Internal $580; CD-RW disk $25	www.ricohdms.com/welco me.html

the capacity of your server's hard drive. Although these backup systems usually come packaged with backup software, the software may not necessarily be compatible with your network operating system. Confirm with the manufacturer that it is compatible before making the investment. Find out, too, whether the software requires that you install your tape backup system on a workstation or the server.

Lastly, be certain that your software is capable of not only backing up your data and program files, but also critical operating system files that contain login information and access rules on all users who access the system.

To understand fully the critical issues involved with server-based backup utilities and the access rights that are necessary to back up all files and directories, consult a network operating system specialist.

Creating Backup Copies of Disks

Under certain circumstances, it is a good idea to make backup copies of programs and data you store on disks.

This improves your chances of disaster recovery if you accidentally lose or damage the original disk. To make a backup copy of a disk using Windows 95, follow these steps:

1. Place the original disk into the floppy disk drive.
2. Double-click on the **My Computer** icon from our desktop.
3. When the My Computer window opens, click on the [A:] icon.
4. Click on **File|Copy** Disk.
5. When the Copy Disk window opens, click on **Start**. Windows 95 copies the files from your disk into the computer's memory and then prompts you to insert the disk to which you want the files copied.
6. Remove the original disk and insert a blank, formatted diskette into the floppy disk drive.
7. Click **OK**. Windows 95 copies the files onto the new disk.

Using Windows 95 Backup to Backup Files

Windows 95 comes packaged with a backup program that enables you to back up files on your hard disk. You can back up to floppy disks or other devices, such as internal tape drives, an external hard drive, or another computer on your network. Once you have completed backing up your files, Windows 95 also helps you restore them if your original files become lost or destroyed. Other Windows 95 backup programs are available at computer stores or online at *www.windows95.com/apps/backup.html*.

To back up your files using Windows 95, follow these steps:

1. Click on **Start** and then point to **Programs|Acc-essories|System Tools.**
2. Click on **Backup.** This opens the Windows 95 Backup window.
3. Click on the files and folders you want to back up.
4. Click **Next Step.**
5. Select a destination for the backup (the floppy drive, or any external drive you connected).
6. Click **Start Backup.** If you are using floppy disks, insert new disks as the system requests them.

To restore data from your backup disks to your hard drive, click on the **Restore** tab in the Backup window. When restoring data, the backup program prompts you if you try to overwrite an existing file. Make sure that you don't overwrite something you intended to save.

Backing Up Large Files to Disk

When you have a large data file or program on a hard drive that you would like to back up to floppy disks, you have to use a utility that is capable of splitting the file into chunks that will fit within the disk's 1.44MB capacity. FileSplit, a shareware program developed by Joseph Partridge, works particularly well for this operation.

You can also use FileSplit to move large files from one PC to another. For example, if you download a 5MB file onto your home PC and you want to install it on your PC at work, you can use FileSplit to copy the 5MB file to four floppy disks and then carry the disks to work with you. This scenario would require that you have FileSplit running at home to split the file and also have it running at work so you can merge the files back together.

> ### What If Your Hard Drive Crashes and You Didn't Back It Up?
>
> Many times it is possible to recover data stored on crashed hard drives. Ontrack Data Recovery Services specializes in such data recovery tasks. You can contact them at 2400 Main Street, Suite 200, Irvine, CA 92714; (800) 872-2599.

You can download a trial version of FileSplit from Partridge's Web site at *www.partridgesoft.com/*. Other file splitting utilities for Windows 95 are available from *www.windows95.com*. Click on the **Utilities** icon and then go to **File Management Utilities** and look for the link leading to File Splitting Utilities.

PROTECTING AGAINST POWER-RELATED PROBLEMS

Personal computers need protection from power interference; for example, momentary rises in voltage and blackouts. Devices called *Uninterruptible Power Supplies* (UPS) and *surge suppressors* are built for this purpose.

UPS (Uninterruptible Power Supply)

For some computers, it is critical that the power be maintained in the event of a power brownout or blackout.

Servers running library automation software are good examples. These systems are continuously opening and closing files. Circulation and/or cataloging data could be lost or corrupted if one of these systems were suddenly to crash because of a blackout.

A backup battery called an *Uninterruptible Power Supply* or *UPS* is used to help insure against this kind of loss. UPSs work like this: Under normal conditions, a UPS supplies power from the wall outlet right to your computer. During a blackout, a device called a *converter* converts the battery's DC power into AC power, which in turn keeps the computer running. The battery backup system gives the operator enough time to shut down the system gracefully before the battery power is exhausted.

How Much Backup Power Do You Need?

Backup power requirements are determined by looking at each hardware component's voltage and amperage requirements and multiplying them to come up with a *VA* rating. If the hardware component is measured in watts, you multiply 1.4 times the number of watts. Use these formulas for determining VA:

Volts x Amperes = VA
Watts x 1.4 = VA

To arrive at the total VA, combine all the VAs for all the hardware components you want protected. The total VA determines the power requirement for your UPS.

What Should You Look for When Buying a UPS?

When you shop around for a UPS, be sure to look for these basic features:

- At least five minutes of runtime at full load
- Automatic shutdown using power management software for longer outages
- Replaceable batteries
- Protection against surge damage
- Audible alarms when battery is on, low, or overloaded

What Is a Surge Suppressor?

PCs face other power anomalies besides blackouts; for example, surges and line noise. A *surge* is an increase in the voltage normally powering your PC. Surges ordinarily occur when your equipment with motors turn off and the energy they were consuming is suddenly sent elsewhere as excess voltage. *Line noise* can be introduced into your system when you turn on fluorescent lights, for example. *Surge suppressors* are devices that help protect your PCs and data lines from these dangers. Most surge suppressors look like power strips and they range in price from $20 to $200.

Resource Tip

QUICKPICK 4.1 is a program that helps you calculate system load when determining which size UPS to purchase. Versions for Windows 3.1 and Windows 95 can be found on the CD-ROM that accompanies this book. Look in the folder labeled MISC.

What Features Should You Look for in a Surge Suppressor?

Look for these features when you shop around for a surge suppressor:

- **330 Volt Let-through**—Underwriters Laboratories (UL) tests surge suppressors and rates them according to how much voltage they let through. UL established 330 volt let-through as the benchmark.
- **High Joule Ratings (or Surge Amp Ratings)**—Joule ratings measure how well your surge suppressor absorbs surges. A rating of 200 to 600 joules is considered acceptable. A rating over 500 joules is exceptional.
- **Internal Fuse**—An internal fuse can break the circuit when a surge of power lasts longer than the surge suppressor is designed to withstand.
- **Modem Protection**—For PCs equipped with modems, look for a suppressor with both modem and AC protection in one unit.
- **Noise Filters**—Noise filters help eliminate electro-magnetic interference.

You can find additional information on UPSs and surge suppressors by consulting any one of the sites listed in Table 1–2.

Table 1–2: Web sites with information on power protection products

Company	Web Address
American Power Conversion	www.apcc.com/
Best Power	www.bestpower.com
Deltec Electronics	www.deltecpower.com/
Panamax	www.panamax.com/
Tripp Lite	tripplite.com

HOW DO YOU MAKE AN EMERGENCY STARTUP DISK?

The last topic I address in this section on disaster recovery is emergency startup disks. Whenever you install a new PC or upgrade one that you currently have, make sure that you create an emergency startup disk to file away for safekeeping in the PC's hardware file. An *emergency startup disk* is a disk that contains important system files used for booting up your PC when you have to bypass booting from the hard drive. Startup disks come in handy if you have to boot your system with a clean system disk because the hard drive is infected with a virus.

The simplest procedure for making an emergency startup disk is to copy the MS-DOS system files and command interpreter from the hard drive (C:\) to a floppy disk (A:\). You do this in DOS by typing the following command at the C:\ prompt:

format a:/s

Transferring Important Program Files to the Startup Disk

You may find it advantageous, from a security standpoint, to transfer certain program files to your startup disk. These are files that hackers can and will use to hack your system if the files are left accessible on the hard drive. Create another backup disk labeled **DOS Backup Files** and save these files to that disk. Once you are finished, delete them from your hard drive.

attrib.exe—sets file attributes (more on this in Chapters 3 and 5)

debug.exe—displays and edits binary code

deltree.exe—deletes directories and all the files and subdirectories contained therein

dosshell.exe—creates a graphical DOS interface

edit.com and *edlin.exe*—DOS text editors that enable you to create, edit, and save files.

format.exe and *unformat.exe*—formats and unformats disks

sys.com—creates startup disks

undelete—recovers files deleted in DOS

Procedures for creating a more thorough DOS/Windows 3.x emergency startup disk are included with the CD-ROM that accompanies this book. Look in the TEXT directory for a file named *BOOT.DOC*.

Making a Startup Disk in Windows 95

Startup disks in Windows 95 are made in the Control Panel. Insert a blank diskette into drive A:\ or drive B:\. To get to the Control Panel, click on the **Start** button, choose **Settings|Control Panel**, and then click on the **Add/ Remove Programs** icon. Lastly, click on the **Startup Disk** tab and then on the **Create Disk** button. Follow the instructions provided in the dialog box.

Windows 95 may also contain some of the same program files listed above (*deltree.exe, debug.exe*, etc.). Look in the C:\WINDOWS\COMMAND\ subdirectory for any files that you may want to transfer to a backup disk and then delete them from the hard drive so they are out of the hacker's reach.

Emergency Booting in Windows 95

If you cannot start Windows95 from your emergency boot disk, copy the file *MSDOS.SYS* from the root directory of your hard disk onto the boot disk and reboot. This file tells DOS where the Windows95 directory can be found.

Chapter 2

Writing and Implementing Security Policies, Standards, and Procedures

Security is mortals' chiefest enemy.
—from Shakespeare's *Macbeth*

After reading Chapter 1, you may have come to the conclusion that the only safe computer in your system is a computer that is unplugged and locked in a storage closet where no one can get at it. The problem is that a computer in that state is useless. In this chapter, I show you how computer security policies can help you achieve security and at the same time put your PCs to good use.

WHAT IS A COMPUTER SECURITY POLICY?

A computer security policy defines which aspects of your computer system you want to protect and outlines a general approach to dealing with security problems. The policy is practical in nature and addresses issues in general terms. Your computer security policy shouldn't detail *how* to protect your computers and data; that is the role of standards and procedures.

WHAT ARE STANDARDS AND PROCEDURES?

Standards are statements that usually include the words *shall* or *will*. They are the activities or rules that support your security policy. For example, if your policy states that personnel records are confidential, your standards may state that personnel records stored to disk *shall* be encrypted. The procedures then spell out in detail how the standards will be implemented. In this example, the procedures would provide step-by-step instructions on how to encrypt personnel files.

Although standards usually are included in a security policy, procedures are kept separate. Procedures can be lengthy and involved and subsequently are developed over a longer period. Standards that typically are included in security policies address these issues:

- Physical security, including security against theft, accidents, and natural disasters
- Application security, such as limiting who can install new software, or limiting access to certain applications through the use of menu systems
- Access control, such as assigning unique user IDs to each user and asking each user to establish a password (in multi-user systems)

- Data security, including backup and using anti-virus software

WHY DO YOU NEED A SECURITY POLICY?

Security policies exist for several reasons. Some of the most important are these:

- To ensure that no one is denied access to your organization's shared resources and services
- To increase everyone's awareness of the responsibilities involved when using personal computers and to explain the disciplinary actions that will be taken for inappropriate use
- To ensure that processes exist for repairing damage to systems while keeping disruption of services to a minimum
- To protect data from unauthorized access or change

WHAT SHOULD BE INCLUDED IN YOUR POLICY?

At the very least, your computer security policy should address two issues: (1) Who is in charge and what are the person's responsibilities, and (2) What are the consequences of misusing the system?

Who Is in Charge?

For security reasons, there is a real advantage to having centralized control of your system, if your organization can support it. Here are three good reasons to put one person in charge:

1. When all the responsibility rests on one person's shoulders, the chances are better that he or she will do a more thorough job.
2. Certain tasks won't go undone because of uncertainty about who is responsible.
3. Everyone who uses your system will know who to go to when they have questions or something goes wrong.

If your system is large enough to warrant a full-time system administrator, he or she is the one who will carry out your organization's security policy. For example, if your security policy requires the monthly updating of your antivirus software, the system administrator does that. Backing up files, managing passwords, and training users are all part of that individual's responsibilities.

In smaller organizations, such as rural libraries, these tasks are the responsibility of the director, the reference librarian, or a number of other individuals who all share in the responsibility. I have worked in systems such as this and even in the best of situations where implementation training had been thorough, there was an element of confusion present when disaster struck. In the case of blackouts, for example, some individuals remembered what their responsibilities were (or at least remembered where to find them in writing), while others panicked and did nothing.

What Is the Orange Book?

The real title, *Trusted Computer System Evaluation Criteria*, is a U.S. Department of Defense publication. It standardizes security system requirements and defines four broad categories of security. Each of these categories is further broken down into more specific classes of security with specific criteria for each. You can view a copy of this document at *www.cs.cmu.edu/afs/cs.cmu.edu/user/bsy/security/CSC-STD-001–83.txt*.

What Are the Responsibilities?

The person in charge should conduct the risk analysis and install safeguards that will help your organization recover from disasters. The most important responsibility in planning for disasters would be to ensure that critical data is being backed up periodically, that each PC has an emergency startup disk on file, and that all the backup power supply systems are in place and working properly. Other responsibilities that should be addressed include:

- Training staff
- Participation in the writing of policies, standards, and procedures
- Monitoring violations
- Maintaining equipment
- Updating software, including anti-virus software, secure menu systems, and file-locking systems
- Maintaining hardware and software files

WHAT HAPPENS WHEN SOMEONE BREAKS THE RULES?

Penalties for violating your security policy may range from temporarily suspending or restricting privileges to prosecution and/or civil actions depending on the severity of the violation. In many organizations, procedures are already in place for referring these matters to other designated officials.

In addition to stating who is in charge, what the individual's responsibilities are, and the consequences of breaking the rules, your general policy statement might also address these other broad issues:

- Who is permitted to use the facilities? For example, faculty, staff, and students only?
- Should no one be permitted to use an account except the person to whom the account was issued?
- What can the computers be used for? For example, instructional and research use only; no private or personal use?
- What is not permitted? For example, stealing passwords, corrupting files, changing program settings, installing personal software?
- Which information resources need to be protected?
- Who does the policy affect?

HOW DO YOU IMPLEMENT SECURITY POLICIES AND PROCEDURES?

Implementing security policies takes a certain amount of planning just as creating them does. You can begin by setting your priorities and drafting a schedule for implementation. If necessary, include in your implementation plan additional details on how certain security problems might be addressed.

As stated earlier, the security *procedures* explain in detail the precise steps your organization takes to protect itself. Some procedures can be automated, such as scanning floppy disks for viruses, automating scheduled scanning of your hard drive, and running automated tape backups. Many other services, however, will depend on people.

In my own practice, I have used job descriptions to implement the procedural aspects of computer security policies. For example, if the computer security policy states as one of its standards that all PCs will run anti-virus software, the responsibility for implementing that procedure is detailed in an individual's job description. When software installation and update procedures are complicated and vary from one machine to the next, the step-by-step procedures can be written down and stored either in a procedure manual or in the information file associated with a particular computer. This two-part system—making references in job descriptions and storing procedures in equipment files—works well over time because references made in job descriptions and written procedures remain intact, although individual employees may come and go.

WHAT ARE THE TRAINING REQUIREMENTS?

The best written policy is useless if the staff members who are supposed to follow it are not aware of it or do not have the proper training to implement it. The amount and type of training employees receive depends on their level of understanding about computer security and what their responsibilities are within the organization. In the section that follows, I describe four levels of training that should accommodate most situations. It is always a good idea to brief new employees on your security policies and procedures.

Free Security Posters

The National Computer Security Center offers eight different security posters free of charge. Just call 1–800–688–6115.

---

1. **Awareness Training**—Applicable to most employees, awareness training explains basic concepts behind computer security practices and raises everyone's awareness about the kinds of threats that exist and shows them which parts of the system are vulnerable. It can also explain why there is a need to protect hardware, software, and data in your organization. The sample "Awareness Training" handout, shown in Figure 2–1, addresses how to select a password.

2. **Management Training**—Your administrative staff should be trained in computer security principles so they can make informed policy decisions. Some of the training resources that are available include:

   • The Computer Security Institute (CSI) and the National Computer Security Association (NCSA) offer training through conferences, seminars, and publications. For more information, contact:

Computer Security Institute (CSI)
600 Harrison Street
San Francisco, CA 94107
Telephone: 415 905–2370
FAX: 415 905–2218
E-mail: *csi@mfi.com*
Web: *www.gocsi.com/csi/*

National Computer Security
  Association (NCSA)
10 S. Courthouse Avenue
Carlisle, PA 17013
Telephone: 717 258–1816
FAX: 717 243–8642
E-mail: *74774.1326@Compuserve.com*
Web: www.ncsa.com/

- Library-specific training can be obtained from ICONnect, a technology initiative of the American Association of School Librarians (AASL). ICONnect offers online courses in Internet basics and advanced courses at *www.ala.org/ ICONN/index.html.*
- Diane K. Kovacs, president of Kovacs Consulting of Brunswick, Ohio, offers workshops on a number of different topics including *Policy, Security and Training: Management of Public Internet Access in Schools, Libraries and Cyber-Cafes.* You can learn more at Kovacs Consulting home page *www.kovacs.com/managing. html.*

3. **Risk Assessment Training**—This level of training teaches library staff to recognize and assess poten-

tial threats to their computer facilities. When such threats are recognized, management can set security requirements that implement school and library security policies; and

4. **Implementation Training**—This level of training provides the appropriate staff with the skills and knowledge necessary to execute computer security procedures and practices. If your organization uses contingency planning, include emergency response, backup, and recovery training. This level of training may require additional training in using specialized applications. An excellent source of information on technical education relating to Microsoft products is located at *www.microsoft.com/iis/default.asp*. Click on the link labeled **Search for a Technical Education Center.** You can search this training database by company name, course name, or you can browse through course offerings organized by state.

Resource Tip

CSI (*www.gocsi.com*) is a San Francisco-based association of computer security professionals. CSI provides a wide variety of information and education programs that are designed to help organizations protect their data.

PASSWORD MANAGEMENT

Passwords are the first line of defense in a strong security system. For this reason, you may want to make password management a part of your overall security policy. In its simplest application, the policy could force members of your staff to change their passwords at periodic intervals (at least once every six months) and state who, if anyone, can share their passwords with others. Everyone should be given a set of rules for password selection. Sample guidelines are presented in Figure 2–1.

Although the best phrases for passwords are random gibberish, it is important to create a password that you can remember without writing it down. Hackers hope that you choose a password that is so difficult to remember that you write it down on a Post-It note and attach it to the bottom of your keyboard. One system you can use to create easy-to-remember-but-difficult-to-crack passwords is to use the first letter of each word in a favorite line of poetry. For example, in Keats' "Oh Solitude" the opening line reads, "Oh Solitude! if I must with thee dwell." When you take the first letter of each word and string them together you create a password something like OSiImwtd. It is gibberish and doesn't exist in any dictionary, but is quite easy to remember. Really, you could apply this to any sentence and create a complex, uncrackable password. For example, "May I borrow 2 cups of sugar?" becomes MIb#2cos?

Another idea is to apply something known as *concatenation*—linking words together that normally aren't linked, such as theala (as in "the American Library Association") or woodsoup. Both of these concatenations would be impervious to a dictionary attack.

To prevent your password from being successfully cracked, you should follow the guidelines presented in Figure 2–1.

Raising Security Awareness
Password Selection

- Never give your password to anyone else.

- Change your password often.

- Change your password immediately after receiving a new account.

- Your password should be between six and eight characters long. Passwords that have fewer than six characters are easier to guess using brute-force attacks.

- Include mixed case, punctuation, and numbers in passwords. This greatly expands the range of possible passwords and makes them harder to guess.

- Do not use anything related to your real name, userID, lover's name, birthday, child's name, pet's name, or anything else anyone could find out about you.

- Do not use passwords that consist entirely of numbers or all one letter.

- Never use English or foreign words. The first thing attackers do is try every word in a dictionary.

- Don't use the same password for network logins, screen savers, and other applications. Hackers know that people have a tendency to use the same password for everything. So if a hacker cracks one of your passwords, it may reveal your other passwords.

Figure 2–1: Awareness training handout on password selection

A SAMPLE SECURITY POLICY

The sample security policy presented in this section shows you that a well-written policy doesn't have to be long and complicated in order to be effective. This sample policy includes the basic policy statements and standards needed to protect your organization from the majority of malicious attacks and other threats to data security. For your convenience in adapting this policy to your situation, a plain ASCII text version is included on the CD-ROM that accompanies this book. Look in the TEXT directory for the file named *POLICY1.DOC*.

COMPUTER SECURITY POLICY

I. **Purpose**

The purpose of this document is to establish a policy for protecting the <Your Organization's Name> computer resources; assign responsibilities for implementing procedures; and establish penalties for malicious attacks, misuse, and/or theft of computer resources.

II. **Scope**

This policy applies to all public-access computers, staff computers, library data, and software. (If your organization supports external online services, you may want to add that those services are subject to the guidelines of the vendor. Also, licensing agreements and copyrighted software are governed by the terms and conditions of the resource contracts and copyright laws.)

III. General Policy Statements

1. It is the responsibility of the system administrator to implement this policy including staff training, monitoring violations, updating software, maintaining hardware and software files, and making recommendations to management for changes in policy.

2. Only faculty, staff, and students are permitted to use the computing facilities. (This will vary depending on your mission.)

3. No one is permitted to use an account except the person to whom it is issued. (Applicable in multi-user systems.)

4. Computers are for instructional and research purposes only. No one may use the computers for private or personal use. (Again, this may vary depending on your mission.)

5. All computerized data is considered to be an asset of the < Your Organization's Name> and shall be protected from theft, damage, corruption, and misuse.

6. Penalties for violating this security policy range from temporary suspension or restriction of privileges to prosecution and/or civil actions. (If the offender is someone on a public library staff, procedures to be followed are ordinarily covered in the library's "Disciplinary Actions Policy"; procedures for handling student offenses may be addressed in a student's "Code of Conduct"; and if the offender is a faculty member, his/her supervisor may make recommendations for punishment to the appropriate administrator.)

IV. Policy Standards

1. Virus protection software will be installed on all personal computers. It shall be updated whenever new releases and/or signature file updates are made available, configured so that it automatically loads into memory, and configured to automatically check floppy disks for viruses.

2. All of the <Your Organization's Name> hardware shall run through surge suppressors.

3. All public-access PCs will be made secure at boot-up.
   This shall include:
   - making emergency boot-up disks that are write-protected for all PCs and storing them in their respective information files
   - instituting password protection at power-up
   - instituting password protection for CMOS set-up
   - storing power-up and CMOS passwords in the associated computer's information file
   - setting public-access PCs to boot from drive C instead of the floppy disk drive
   - disabling the boot-up break-in keys F5 and F8

4. All public-access PCs shall be made secure after boot-up. This shall include:
   - installing secure menu systems that prevent users from accessing DOS, Windows 3.x Program Manager, or the Windows 95 Desktop
   - making important system files and executables "Read Only" and "Hidden"

5. Data stored on servers (bibliographic and circulation records in the case of libraries, and student

records in the case of schools) shall be backed up to tape daily and stored off-site.

6. The <Your Organization's Name> server shall be powered by an Uninterruptible Power Supply (UPS) and secured from unauthorized access physically and via the network.

7. All public access PCs, keyboards, monitors, and peripherals shall be physically secured with cables and padlocks

---

Security Policy Templates

If you want more information on writing security policies, you might consider purchasing the security templates offered by Baseline Software, Inc. "Information Security Policies Made Easy" by Charles Cresson Woods includes over 800 already-written information security policies in book form and on CD-ROM. For information on price and related issues, go to Baseline Software, Inc.'s site at *www.baselinesoft.com/*.

SAMPLE SECURITY AND ACCEPTABLE USE POLICIES

The online policy archives listed in Table 2–1 are accessible on the Internet. These archives will be useful for drafting security policies for academic, corporate, private, and public libraries, as well as for schools and small businesses.

Table 2–1: Sources of security and acceptable use policies

Title	Location
Acceptable Use of Information Systems at Virginia Tech	www.vt.edu/policies/ accepentuseguide.html
Security policies from the Department of Commerce and the Office of Management and Budget	csrc.ncsl.nist.gov/ secplcy/
MU's Collection of Computing Policies	www.missouri.edu/ policy/copies/
Computers and Academic Freedom Archive	www.eff.org/CAF/

Chapter 3

All about Hackers and Hacking

Hacking is the art of attempting everything until something finally works.
—Anonymous (from *How to Hack UNIX System V*)

Chapter 3 takes a different approach to PC security. Instead of just telling you that hackers are a problem, this chapter takes you inside their world and shows you why the problem exists. By understanding what hackers do and how they think, you can make more informed decisions about how to secure your PCs.

Chapter 3 focuses on some of the better known cookbook methods hackers use to break into public-access PCs. It doesn't go into the details of what hackers do once they break into your system; that would vary greatly from site-to-site depending on which services are available.

There is a certain danger in making this kind of information readily available. The possibility exists that a reader may use maliciously some of the ideas presented in this chapter. It is more important, however, for teachers and librarians to become aware of the potential risks they face. What better way to bring attention to these risks than to present real-life hacking scenarios? Yes, hackers can create security problems, but the problems exist because operating systems like Windows and DOS and applications like Netscape Navigator ship in insecure states.

WHO ARE THE HACKERS?

Hackers are an interesting lot. Some of the older ones are heroes; some are in jail. They have their own jargon, jokes, and myths. *The New Hacker's Dictionary*, conceived and edited by Eric S. Raymond, defines a hacker as, "a person who enjoys exploring the details of programmable systems and how to stretch their capabilities, as opposed to most users, who prefer to learn only the minimum necessary." (See *www.ccil.org/jargon/jargon_toc.html* for an online version of *The New Hacker's Dictionary*.)

A general misconception is to think that hackers spend all of their time breaking into systems and stealing or destroying sensitive information. Most hackers simply enjoy digging into computer systems and figuring out what makes them tick.

Resource Tip

Phrack Magazine at *freeside.com/phrack.html* provides the hacker community with information on operating systems, networking technologies, telephony, and other topics of interest to the international computer underground.

WHAT IS HACKING?

Hacking is what hackers do. Hacking is learning about operating systems and all of the subtle nuances of the computers and the applications they run. The rogues have made a bad name for the good hackers. These bad guys break into systems to do damage. Although hackers like Kevin Mitnik are reputed to make a practice of destroying and altering data, the good guys do not threaten you and they do not intentionally damage your system.

The Electronic Frontier Foundation

Some hackers break the law; the majority do not. State and federal law enforcers don't always distinguish between the two. The EFF (Electronic Frontier Foundation) was established to protect the civil liberties of legitimate computer users and to provide a legal defense for those who have been victimized. You can access EFF's home page at *www.eff.org*.

WHO HACKS SCHOOLS AND LIBRARIES?

Fortunately, schools and libraries aren't being attacked by techno hackers (high-tech computer operators who use computers to engage in criminal activities). They are, however, the target of amateur hackers. The problems amateurs create for schools and libraries include interruption of service, virus attacks, password cracking, and general messing around with program settings. I've found that the best line of defense against amateur hackers is to think the way they think. For best results, you should learn not only how they hack, but understand why they hack.

WHY DO HACKERS HACK PUBLIC ACCESS COMPUTERS?

Hackers go after public-access PCs for various reasons, but the biggest reason is to test their skills at bypassing security measures. Their motivation for bypassing a secure menu system, for example, may be ultimately to get at programs or services that are more interesting or useful to them—at least more interesting than what the school or library's menu system has to offer. In other cases, hackers break-in to systems just to be "kewl" ("cool" in hacker speak) and to impress their friends.

In rare instances, hackers have used PC-based systems to get back at someone—to seek revenge *hacker style*. They get back at libraries or library employees by loading viruses into library PCs, deleting programs and data, or by launching "denial of service" attacks on servers linked to the Internet. In schools, some hackers seek revenge against their peers by breaking into a shared network and resetting restrictions on a particular user's account or by deleting files in that person's directory.

TIP

The Fishcam Secret - This isn't really a hack, but it is fun. Try pressing CTRL+ALT+F (CTRL+Option+F on Macs) while you are running Netscape to see the second oldest live camera site on the Web: Lou Montulli's fishtank.

COOKBOOK METHODS OF ATTACKING PCS

In this section, I explore common exploits that hackers use to take advantage of loopholes found in DOS, Windows, and various programs. Each attack scenario offers countermoves and fixes and provides you with a sense of how hackers think and operate. If you are the person in charge of PC security in your organization, you can use this section to help prepare a defense against future attacks.

Attack Scenario #1: Cracking CMOS

Bootup and setup passwords. CMOS passwords offer a basic level of protection for your computer. Bootup password protection begins the moment you turn on your machine. The bootup process stops and will not resume until you enter the proper password. The other level of CMOS password protection requires that you enter a password to gain access to the CMOS setup screens that are basic to the operation of your computer hardware.

Who will get there first? If you do not set a password to gain access to CMOS, you risk the chance of an unauthorized individual going in and tampering with essential system configuration and/or setting up their own password. Worse yet, mischievous individuals who can gain access to your CMOS setup will also go in and password protect your computer's power-up, which renders your computer useless. (The availability of CMOS password protection is dependent on the BIOS chip in the computer. Not all computers offer power-up password protection.)

Breaking into the case. Hackers cannot do much if you've locked them out with a power-up password. The only way a hacker could gain access to your system through this security lock is by opening up the case and somehow disabling, or shorting-out the CMOS battery. The hacker will also look at the motherboard to see whether there's a jumper to reset the BIOS. If the CMOS battery isn't soldered in place, a hacker may try removing it for 15 to 30 minutes and then reinstalling it in an attempt to dump the PC's static CMOS memory. There might also be a jumper wire to which an external replacement battery has been attached. A case lock, like those described in Chapter 4, can keep hackers away from your CMOS battery.

Cracking CMOS passwords. If you password protect CMOS setup, but forget the password; or a denizen of the underworld sets it for you before you can, you can run an application called KiLLCMOS to reset your computer's CMOS settings to the factory defaults. You can find KiLLCMOS at various software archives on the Net. Try using an Archie server (see *www.cris.com/~acbenson)* and search on the text strings *kcmos32i.zip* for Windows or *killcmos.zip* for DOS.

Using password catchers. Hackers might also get at your password with a *password catcher* or *key logger.* CMOS password catchers retrieve the password last used on your motherboard. Different catchers work with different motherboards, and it can be a hit-and-miss operation finding one that works. You can use this tool yourself if you happen to forget your CMOS setup password. Here are three programs you can try:

Program Name	File name
AMI BIOS Password Decoder	Amidecod.zip
Award BIOS Password Decoder	awardpsw.zip
Award BIOS Password Cracker	aw.zip

Warning

On two different occasions I touched a PC's outer case and felt a static electric shock, which in turn wiped out the CMOS settings. Luckily, the first time this happened I had two PCs that were exactly alike and I simply copied the system information from one PC to the other. From that point forward, I printed the CMOS setup screens and filed them in each individual PC's hardware file. The second time I "zapped" a PC, I was able to reconfigure CMOS based on the setup files I had saved and stored in that particular PC's file.

Use Archie to find an FTP site on the Net that stores one of these files.

Know Your Enemy

2600: The Hacker Quarterly (*www.2600.com*) is a magazine devoted to hackers and the computer underground.

Attack Scenario #2: Breaking into MS-DOS

Creating an embedded object in Word. Some applications are designed in such a way that they provide the hooks needed to access the operating system. In one of the local school labs, a student asked his teacher whether he could print files from DOS. The teacher in charge said no because the lab policy stated that no one could access the operating system for any reason. The PCs were running a secure menu system and MS-Word was included among the various menu choices. Not a minute had passed and the student was in DOS without having knowledge of the school's menu system password. Here's how he did it:

1. First he opened a new MS Word document. (He could have opened an existing file. This trick would have worked either way.)
2. On the Insert pull-down menu, he clicked **Object**.
3. When the Object window appeared, he clicked on the **Create from File** tab.
4. He entered the file name **C:\command.com** in the file name dialog box.
5. Then he selected the **Display As Icon** check box to display the object as an icon.
6. Next he clicked **OK** and a DOS icon appeared embedded in the Word document.
7. When he double-clicked the DOS icon, a DOS window opened.

This works in Windows 3.x and Windows 95 using Word or WordPad.

> ## Warning
>
> WinNuke is an application that launches a denial of service attack affecting Windows 95 and other Windows-based systems. To test your vulnerability, go to site *www.darkening.com/winnuke/demo.html* and click on the vulnerability check. If you're vulnerable and you'd like an actual demonstration of what it is like being WinNuked, this Web site gives you the opportunity to "Nuke" yourself.

Attack Scenario #3: Using Microsoft Office to Run Shells

The friendlier the programs, the greater your risks. Hackers also can get to DOS or run Windows shells from Microsoft Office products. This is risky because once a hacker gains this level of access, he has a good shot at disabling your security devices. Here's how he does it:

1. He clicks on the **Help** pull-down menu and then chooses **About Microsoft Word,** or **About Microsoft Excel,** or **About Microsoft Powerpoint**—whichever program happens to be running.
2. He clicks on the button labeled **System Info.** This opens a system information window.
3. One of the buttons on the toolbar in this window is labeled **Run.** When he clicks on this button, the Run Application Window opens.

The hacker can then enter the name of any executable program he wants to run and then click on **OK.** He could enter *command.com* to access DOS, for example; or he can choose one of the text editors or shells offered right before his eyes. The Run Application window says, "Select the application you want to run." Listed among the choices are Control Panel, Notepad, System Configuration Editor (which is linked to the *sysedit.exe* file located in the C:\WINDOWS\SYSTEM subdirectory), Registry Editor, Wordpad and Explorer. He simply makes his choice and clicks OK.

Locking program files. The simplest defense against hackers running programs such as *command.com, control.exe, explorer.exe, notepad.exe, poledit.exe, progman.exe, regedit.exe, sysedit.exe, taskman.exe, winfile.exe,* and *write.exe* is to place locks on these applications. PC Security (a file-locking application included on the CD-ROM that accompanies this book) and other file-locking applications discussed in Chapter 7, enable you to place locks on executable files. Other alternatives are to move the programs to a floppy disk or rename them so hackers cannot easily recognize them.

Attack Scenario #4: Breaking into Windows 95

Password protect Windows 95. According to Windows Help, the way to secure a Windows 95 PC that is not connected to a network is as follows:

1. Go to Control Panel and click on **Network Properties**. Click on the **Configuration** tab and set the **Primary Network Logon** option to **Windows Logon**. (*Note*: The steps in this section may vary for your computers, depending on the version of Windows 95 you are running and the options you have installed.)

2. On the **Access Control** tab, click **Share-Level Access Control**.
3. Next, change the password and customize preferences and desktop settings. You do this by opening Control Panel and clicking on **Passwords Properties**; then choose the Change Passwords tab and click Change Windows Password.
4. On the **User Profiles** tab, click **Users can customize their preferences and desktop settings**.
5. Rebooting completes the process of password protecting your Windows 95 machine.
6. Now a Welcome to Windows message comes up, asking you to enter your user name and password to log on to Windows. A second window pops up, asking you to confirm the password you entered.

Breaking through the password protection. A hacker looks at this logon screen, clicks the Cancel button, and logs on as the Default user. The password-protected logon information is used primarily for remote file sharing and desktop preferences. So much for password protection.

The logon passwords are saved in the *.pwl* files stored in the Windows directory. The *.pwl* file names correspond with the logon name of the user. For example, if I set up a password with the logon name **acbenson**, the corresponding password file located in the Windows directory is named *acbenson.pwl*.

Disabling passwords. The hacker disables passwords by renaming the *.pwl* files. For example, the hacker types **rename acbenson.pwl acbenson.pw_** at the C:\WINDOWS> prompt. Now after the machine reboots, the hacker is prompted for a new password. If the hacker enters a new user name, too, Windows 95 politely asks, "Would you like this computer to retain your individual settings for use when you log on here in the future?" If the hacker answers yes, Windows saves the customized preferences and desktop settings he entered.

Disabling password protection. Hackers may forgo performing the above operations and instead shut the machine off and turn it back on. As soon as the screen says "Loading Windows 95," they hit the F8 key, which brings up the Microsoft Windows 95 Startup Menu along with several different startup options. They then choose Safe mode and when the computer finishes booting up, they run regedit (Registry editor) and make whatever changes to the system they wish.

Restrict access to Windows 95 Desktop. You can establish one line of defense against hackers messing with password files by implementing the Systems Restrictions policy. You can do this by running the System Policy Editor described in Chapter 5. Start the System Policy Editor, click on **File|Open Registry** and then double-click on the **Local User** icon. Next, open the **System|Restrictions** folder, which is shown in Figure 3–1. Disabling the DOS prompt will prevent hackers from erasing the *.pwl* file in that manner.

Going around restrictions with a bootup disk. If you disable access to the DOS prompt after Windows 95 starts, a hacker could boot from a floppy disk and remove both the *.pwl* and *.pol* files. (The data that defines the System Policy Editor restrictions is stored in the *.pol* file.)

Installing a floppy disk lock. If a hacker can boot from a floppy disk and delete the *.pwl* and *.pol* files, any restric-

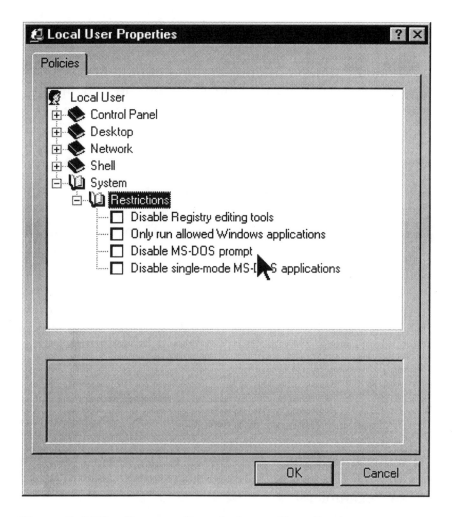

Figure 3–1: The Systems Restriction policy allows you to disable the DOS prompt.

tions you placed on the computer are removed. Installing a floppy disk drive lock would prevent this form of access. These devices are described in Chapter 4. If you wanted to troubleshoot the machine or add new applications, you could do so by simply unlocking the device.

Attack Scenario #5: Messing around with Netscape

Oh boy! They're running Netscape! If you are running Netscape Navigator on a public-access PC, you probably have discovered that hackers love to mess around with the program settings. The first thing they like to do is get rid of that boring home page you have loading and set it to The Infinity Void, which is kewl. And what about that tiresome font? They can change that, too, to something like Comic Sans MS and make the unvisited links purple. In Netscape 3.0, these changes are made under **Options|General Preferences**. In Communicator 4.0, they're made under **Edit|Preferences|Appearance**.

Making the *NETSCAPE.INI* file Hidden and Read-only. The *NETSCAPE.INI* file keeps track of all the various settings in Netscape, such as font, color, and home page. You can usually find a reference to its location in the *WIN.INI* file, for example:

[Netscape]
ini=C:\WINDOWS\netscape.ini

Set your home page, font, colors, etc., to your liking and then make the *NETSCAPE.INI* file Hidden and Read-only. In Windows 3.x and Windows 95, you do this by highlighting the *NETSCAPE.INI* file in File Manager or Windows Explorer, and then choosing **File|Properties** and

Renaming Sensitive Files

Hackers are good at finding and using obscure programs that you may not be aware of, such as the *sysedit.exe* file located in the *C:\WINDOWS* directory. When hackers run *sysedit.exe*, they can edit *autoexec.bat, config.sys, win.ini, system.ini,* etc. Hackers also are good at knowing which executable files are useful hacking tools, such as *taskman.* Your counter offensive is to rename these "useful" files. This still gives you administrative access to the programs because you know what their altered file names are. There are other executables that can be used in a destructive manner; for example, *DELTREE.* These were listed at the end of Chapter 1 as files I recommended you remove to a backup disk rather than leaving them on the hard disk and simply renaming them. Here is a list of files you may want to consider renaming:

C:\WINDOWS\WINHLP32.EXE
C:\WINDOWS\WRITE.EXE
C:\WINDOWS\REGEDIT.EXE
C:\WINDOWS\NOTEPAD.EXE
C:\WINDOWS\WINHELP.EXE
C:\WINDOWS\CONTROL.EXE
C:\WINDOWS\SYSEDIT.EXE
C:\WINDOWS\TASKMAN.EXE
C:\WINDOWS\WINFILE.EXE
C:\WINDOWS\POLEDIT.EXE
C:\WINDOWS\WINPOPUP.EXE

putting check marks in the boxes next to **Read-only** and **Hidden**. Normally you find *NETSCAPE.INI* in the C:\WINDOWS directory.

What about bookmarks? Most everyone will add their favorite bookmarks to your bookmark list. Mischievous characters may change the properties of your library- or school-related bookmarks so that they connect to unexpected sites. You can prevent both of these events from happening by making the *BOOKMARK.HTM* file Hidden and Read-only. The *BOOKMARK.HTM* file is ordinarily found in the Netscape subdirectory.

Removing the Hidden and Read-only attributes. A hacker can remove the **Hidden** and **Read-only** attributes just as easily as you set them. For this defense to be fully effective, you should: (1) Couple it with a secure menu system that prevents hackers from gaining access to these files, and (2) prevent hackers from breaking out of the bootup process. Breaking out of the bootup process, which is addressed in Attack Scenario #7, could make it possible for a hacker to get at the files before any secure menu system even loads.

In summary, the best defense against hackers changing Netscape Navigator's appearance and bookmark list is:

1. Make the *NETSCAPE.INI* and *BOOKMARK.HTM* files **Hidden** and **Read-only**.
2. Install a secure menu system that blocks access to the operating system.
3. Add the command **SWITCH=/N/F** to the *config.sys* file to make it harder for hackers to break out of the bootup process.

Chapter 8 presents a more sophisticated approach to this problem. There you learn how to use a program called a *resource editor* to gray out specific menu items found in Netscape Navigator.

Can Hackers "Hack" Your Web Page?

Yes! In fact, some well-known sites that have been hacked include NASA, the Air Force, the CIA, and Department of Justice. The before and after images of these pages have been archived by *2600 Magazine* at *www.2600.com/hacked_pages/.*

Attack Scenario #6: Breaking into Everybody's Menu

Shutting down the application. No security system is 100 percent secure, especially one that runs under Windows 95. The security flaw presented here is not embedded within Everybody's Menu system (a secure Windows-based menu system developed by CARL Corporation, which is described further in Chapter 5). It results from the platform upon which Everybody's Menu runs: Windows 95.

Let's take a look at what your average hacker-type will do when he or she runs up against Everybody's Menu. One of the first things a hacker will try on a Windows 95 machine is pressing CTRL+ALT+DEL. This might allow the hacker to shut down Everybody's Menu while Windows 95 remains running. If it works, the hacker has free access to your system. If the Start button and Taskbar did not load, the hacker simply presses CTRL+ESC to launch Task Manager. All programs are accessible from the Run menu.

Installing keyboard security. What will your counterattack be? The best defense is to load the application's keyboard security feature during installation. This feature is built right into Everybody's Menu system. This prevents the attacker from using the CTRL+ALT+DEL keys to break out of the program. Check to make sure that this line is written into your *C:\WINDOWS\system.ini* file under the [386Enh] section:

> device=C:\e_menu\NOSYSKEY.386.

You say you did disable warm boots during installation, but then you enabled it because you couldn't use CTRL+ALT+DEL when other applications hung? There's always a tradeoff for such conveniences, and this one can be troublesome. For example, if one of the applications you are running from the menu hangs and CTRL+ALT+DEL is disabled, you may have to do a cold boot to jar it loose. Closing down Windows 95 with applications running means that you will have to run Scandisk before Windows 95 fully boots.

Running Windows 95 in Safe mode. Let's say that you did not disable the keyboard security feature and you've been stopping the hackers dead in their tracks. Then one day a hacker comes along and just hits the reset button and reboots the machine in Safe mode, in which case Everybody's Menu system doesn't load. Next, the hacker clicks on the Start button, chooses **Find|Files or Folders**; finds the *system.ini* file and remarks out the *device=C:\e_menu\NOSYSKEY.386* line by placing a semicolon in front of it. Then the hacker moves on to visit the C:\WINDOWS\StartMenu\Programs\StartUp directory to see what is loading automatically when Windows runs. It doesn't take a genius to guess that the file named *Everybdy.exe* is the file that runs Everybody's Menu Builder, so this is the file the hacker moves or deletes.

Hacking Everybody's Menu Builder. Could it get any worse? Yes! The hacker could be thinking, "Why did those teachers design such a boring looking menu in the first place?" Changing it is easy once the hacker has access to your files. The hacker goes to the Programs menu and chooses Everybody's Menu Builder; loads the program called Menu Builder and changes the screen title from "Welcome to our school" to "Hey lamers! Get a life!" Next, the hacker alters the school library's catalog menu item so instead of linking to the online catalog, it links to *Bubba's Bodacious Babes* Web site.

Hiding and/or locking files. Your last line of defense could be to use one of these techniques, all of which are explained in Chapter 5:

1. Hide the *system.ini* file and the Everybody's Menu Builder executable files using the **attrib** command;
2. Use a stronger defense by renaming the directory so it is not so easily recognized and then altering the file names of the executables in that directory by adding the extended ASCII character ALT+255. (This is an "invisible" character you can create by holding the ALT key down and then pressing 255 on the number pad.)
3. Remove any references to Everybody's Menu Builder from the Start menu programs. Another solution would be to install a file locking application like the ones presented in Chapter 7 and password protect the critical files.

Attack Scenario #7: Re-Setting Windows Wallpaper with Netscape Navigator

Changing Windows wallpaper. Netscape Navigator supports a feature that sets any image found on the Web as the Windows wallpaper. You can access this feature by placing the cursor on an image, right-clicking the mouse, and selecting **Set As Wallpaper.** Young hackers have fun with this one because it takes only two mouse clicks to reset the wallpaper to something that suits their fancy— animated lightening bolts, etc.

Where does the wallpaper file get saved? When you select an image to be used as wallpaper, Navigator saves the image in the Windows directory and then modifies the Windows wallpaper setting to point to this new file. In the 16–bit version of Navigator this file is named *NETSCAPE.BMP*, and in the 32–bit version it is named *Netscape Wallpaper.bmp*.

Setting up roadblocks. This is how you can block a hacker's attempt to change Windows wallpaper: First, choose the wallpaper you like. Second, set the file's properties to **Read-only** and **Hidden.** (If you create your own wallpaper, make sure that you use Navigator's 16–bit or 32–bit file naming conventions as noted in the preceding paragraph.) Once the wallpaper file is set as **Read-only,** Navigator will ignore any attempts to reset the wallpaper.

Attack Scenario #8: Breaking out of the Boot Process in MS-DOS

Bring your own boot disk. Hackers might spend some time trying to crack passwords on menu systems or file locks,

> **Warning**
>
> When you set the wallpaper file as **Read-only**, the 32–bit version of Netscape Navigator 3.0 and 4.0 crashes when someone attempts to reset the wallpaper. Windows 95 continues running, so it is just a matter of restarting Navigator. The 16–bit version of Netscape Navigator simply ignores any attempts to reset the wallpaper.

but more often they'll simply reboot the computer and attempt to break into the boot process before all of the security systems have loaded. Hackers know that PCs ordinarily try to boot from A:\, and if no system files are found on A:\, the PC goes to drive C:\. Hackers can bypass the normal bootup process by inserting their own system disk into the floppy drive just before rebooting the computer. This usually gets them to the system prompt without any problem. Now the hacker can delete files, run programs, or edit your *config.sys* or *autoexec.bat* files so certain security features will not load the next time the computer boots up.

Altering the boot sequence. The simplest way to prevent a hacker from booting off of his or her own system disk is to go into the CMOS Setup program and choose the option that sets the boot sequence at C,A. Be sure that you password protect your CMOS Setup program to prevent a hacker from going in and changing the boot sequence back to A,C. If your BIOS doesn't support the choice of boot drive sequence plus password protection, you might consider using a floppy drive lock. (This is described in Chapter 4.)

Using the F5 or F8 keys. Changing the boot sequence prevents hackers from booting up with their own system disks, but it doesn't prevent them from breaking into the boot process another way. The standard practice is to press the F5 or F8 key just before MS-DOS begins loading. This causes the system to bypass startup commands.

Preventing an F5 or F8 breakout. Not all is lost; you can disable the F5 and F8 keys so hackers cannot use them during bootup. Later versions of MS-DOS make this possible with the **SWITCHES=/N** command. Adding this command line to the *config.sys* file prevents the F5 and F8 keys from working. (This is explained in more detail in Chapter 5.) The **SWITCHES=/N** command does not prevent hackers from breaking into the bootup process with CTRL+Break, however.

What about that CTRL+Break key combination? The best tool for stopping breakouts is a small application that disables the CTRL+Break key combination. These applications are built in to many security utilities and they are also available as stand-alone applications. Three examples of stand-alones are *dsenab11.zip*, *cadel.zip*, and *kystp110.zip*. All three of these can be downloaded from *www.filez.com*. To find these programs at this site, search the Windows and DOS file libraries, using the text string **ctrl-break.**

GateWAY is a security program included with the CD-ROM that accompanies this book. GateWAY password protects your PC and it disables the breakout keys, including CTRL+Break, during bootup. You can find a copy of GateWAY in the MISC directory.

Attack Scenario #9: Playing the Shell Game with IE (Internet Explorer)

Using IE as a Windows 95 shell. Maybe you aren't aware of it, but most newbie hackers know this secret. IE can be used to run any program on your computer. IE is a Windows shell program and hackers can use it as an alternative to the Windows 95 desktop. If you are running a secure menu system, such as Everybody's Menu, and one of the menu buttons cranks up IE and connects you to Electric Library, for example, you might as well just give the hackers your menu password.

Enter C: instead of a URL. Hackers will start IE just as though they were going to connect to the Web. As soon as IE tries to initiate a connection, they kill it by clicking on the stop button. The machine doesn't even have to be connected to the Internet to do this. Next they enter c: in the address box instead of a Web URL and press ENTER. This action displays all of the file folders on the hard drive.

Let's play solitaire. Some hackers may just be out for some fun. They might go to the Windows folder and double-click on *sol.exe* to start up a game of solitaire. Or they may click on the Program Files folder and Accessories and then double-click on *mspaint.exe* to paint a picture. Other hackers may realize that they also have access to DOS and the Registry. Access to *regedit.exe*, which is located in the Windows folder, gives hackers the ability to control the machine. Hackers also can try entering other drive letters in the address box, such as N:, S:, or Z:, etc. If they can gain access to the Registry on a server, they may be able to control the network.

Simplest solution. It goes without saying: the easiest way to fix this problem is to remove IE from our computers. If you are not willing to do this and replace it with something else, run a second line of defense that locks access to all programs except those you want to run. An excellent shareware program described in Chapter 7 that offers this feature is called PC Security. PC Security offers five different security modes. The one named Restricted System allows you to choose which applications are permitted to run and which will be restricted. This way, even if IE is permitted to run, when hackers open IE and browse through folders clicking on programs, they will be met with a message that reads, "This operation has been canceled due to restrictions in effect on this computer. Please contact your system administrator." Yes, some hackers will try to override the security program you are using, but most will give up and go back to surfing the Web.

GUIDELINES FOR DEFENDING AGAINST HACKERS

This is a short summary of the basic defenses presented in this chapter and later in Chapter 5. I divide the various options available into two levels based on cost. The first-level solutions are free and most are obtainable by making simple changes to your operating system files. The second-level defenses utilize commercial third-party security software.

Level One Solutions

- Set the CMOS passwords.
- Add the **SWITCHES=/N/F** command to your *config.sys* file to disable the F5 and F8 breakout keys and remove the two second delay that comes after the "Starting MS-DOS..." message.
- Remove programs that enable users to access DOS or *regedit*.
- Insert restrictions in the *PROGMAN.INI* file.
- Make your *.ini* files read-only and hidden and then remove the *attrib.exe* file from the DOS directory.
- Don't run Internet Explorer.
- Set restrictions with the Windows 95 policy editor.
- Install a freeware password protector for files.

Level Two Solutions

- Install a shareware program that disables the CTRL+Break Key.
- Install Centurion Guard.
- Install a secure menu system, such as WinU or Everybody's Menu.
- Use a resource editor to gray-out menu choices on applications.
- Install a security package that enables you to place restrictions on Windows 95 or Windows 3.x functions, such as Fortres 101.

Chapter 4

Physical Security in Schools and Libraries

Everybody knows if you are too careful you are so occupied in being careful that you are sure to stumble over something.
—Gertrude Stein, *Everybody's Autobiography*, 1937

Protecting your hardware from being stolen or vandalized is known as *physical security*. Physical security can include site security, which controls access to your PCs using door locking or card control systems. You can attain higher levels of security by using *biometrics authentication systems*. These systems prove a person's identity by measuring physical characteristics. Biometrics devices perform various operations including fingerprint reading, retina scanning, and voice analysis.

Most libraries and school labs do not need this level of security. Classroom doors generally are open to everyone and public-access PCs in libraries are out in the open and easy to access. Badging and carding systems are impractical. Access control systems, such as closed-circuit TV cameras, may work well in large institutions, but the cost of these systems typically is high. For these reasons, Chapter 4 focuses only on devices that can be used to restrain hardware physically. This chapter also explains how to restrict access to floppy disk drives and deter vandals from going after your CPUs and memory chips.

Details on ordering products mentioned in this chapter are listed in Table 4–1 at the end of the chapter. This chapter does not cover the question of electrical threats, such as power surges and blackouts, which were covered in Chapter 1.

IMPLEMENTING PHYSICAL SECURITY MEASURES

There are two general approaches to providing physical security for your organization's public access PCs: Physical retention systems and motion detection devices.

Physical Retention Systems

The most basic security system includes devices for locking down your monitor, CPU case, mouse, and keyboard. A complete lock-down system from Innovative Security Products is shown in Figure 4–1. On the back of the CPU case, there is a lid-locking device. This prevents thieves from stealing internal components, such as memory chips, hard drives, and video cards, etc.

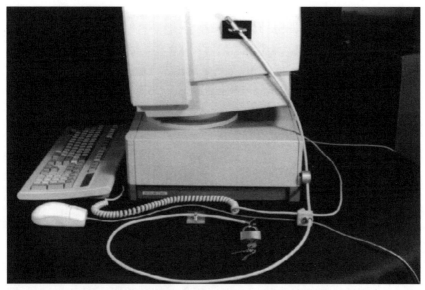

Figure 4–1: Innovative Security Products complete security kit.
Reprinted with permission from Innovative Security Products

The kit also includes two lock-down plates, one fastened to the monitor, and the other anchored to the tabletop. A device called a *cable trap* secures the mouse and keyboard cables. Everything is fastened together with a five-foot length of steel cable, which passes through the lock-down plates, lid lock, and cable trap. One end of the cable is secured with a solid brass padlock.

Steel Cables

Steel cables are generally used to restrain one or more components as a group, such as the PC casing, monitor, and printer at one workstation. Although cables may look intrusive and bulky, they are excellent deterrents and rea-

---

Resource Tip

National Institutes of Health (NIH) at *www.alw.nih.gov/Security/security.html* maintains a list of security-related resources from around the world that provide information about security vulnerabilities, security e-zines, cryptography, Java security, Windows NT, and UNIX security, and much more.

---

sonably priced. A basic system sells for approximately $18 to $25.

Cables pass through retention sockets, adhesive lock-down plates, or other devices that are built into or attached to a component's case. SecurTech Company offers a basic lock-down system called ANYCASE, which is shown in Figure 4–2. ANYCASE is designed to secure PC cases and is comprised of a one-quarter inch diameter cable, two lock-down plates, two cable clamps, and extra rubber feet if you need them.

The SecurTech Company offers another restraining system for monitors, keyboards, and printers, etc., that utilizes devices called RIGHTON Spot Anchors. These anchors, shown in Figure 4–3, come in a variety of styles and are attached to components with a strong adhesive. One series of anchors is designed to attach to plastic surfaces; another is designed to attach to painted metal surfaces; and still another series is designed for components that offer only a narrow surface for attachment, such as keyboards. Spot anchor systems range in price from $14 to $17 depending on the length of the cable.

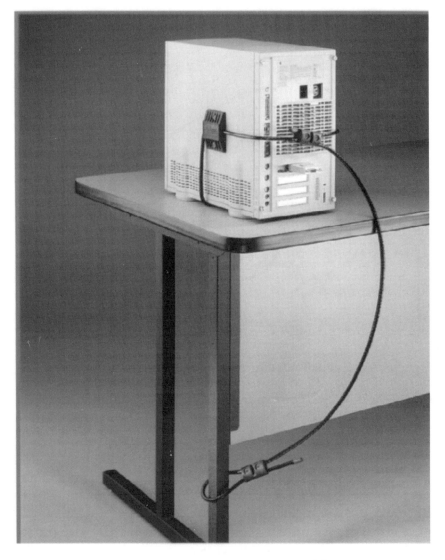

Figure 4–2: SecurTech Company's ANYCASE security system for locking down computers cases to fixed locations.
Reprinted with permission from SecurTech Company

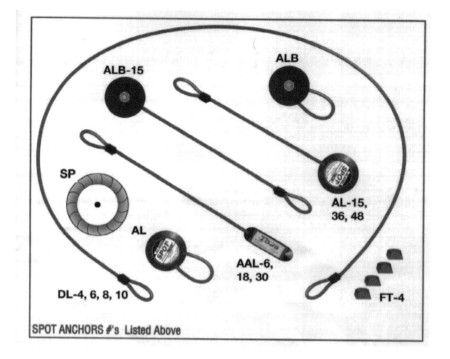

Figure 4–3: SecurTech Company's Spot anchors are used to secure a variety of components including computers, typewriters, VCRs, copy machines, and FAX machines, etc.
Reprinted with permission from SecurTech Company

Adhesive Lock-Down Plates

If there is not a place on your computer component through which you can string a cable, you can provide an anchor by attaching an adhesive *lock-down plate* with an eyelet, as shown in Figure 4–4. These plates can also be attached to a tabletop or other location where you terminate the cable. Keep in mind that once you attach one of these plates to a surface, it is there to stay.

Figure 4–4: Lock-down plate kit consists of steel plates and cyanoacrylic adhesive.
Reprinted with permission from Innovative Security Products.

SecurTech Company offers another anchoring device called TraVlok, which is shown in Figure 4–5. The TraVlok anchor is a self-contained system that includes the anchor and cable. The coated cable is coiled inside the anchor allowing you to remove only as much as you need. TravLock anchor systems cost around $30.

Locking Systems

In order to prevent items from being removed that are restrained with cables, the cable has to be secured at both ends. There are different ways of doing this, but at least one end must be secured with a padlock or other locking

Security Conference

NCSA's Information Security Forum is an online conferencing system that supports general discussions on computer security. Participants range from the general public to experts in the security field. To join in, go to NCSA's home page at *www.ncsa.com* and click on the Web conferencing link.

device. When you use padlocks, you need to keep track of keys or combinations. A good place to store these are in the PC hardware files I discussed in Chapter 1.

Lid-locking devices, such as the one shown in Figure 4–1, are designed to keep thieves from getting inside your CPU case. The Lid Lock 2000, designed by Innovative Security Products, is screwed to the case through one of the original lid screw holes. The locking mechanism is operated with a key.

Motion Detection Devices

Battery-powered alarm systems are available for attaching to the outside of components, such as laptops, PCs, printers, and other office equipment. When an individual tries to move the component, a loud alarm sounds. The Protect-All Alarm system shown in Figure 4–6 is disarmed by setting the two dials to predetermined numbers. You arm the alarm by spinning the dials to different numbers.

Innovative Security Products offers a complete motion detection package that is similar to the system shown in Figure 4–1. The Ultimate Security Kit shown in Figure 4–7 has all of the same components, except the padlock is

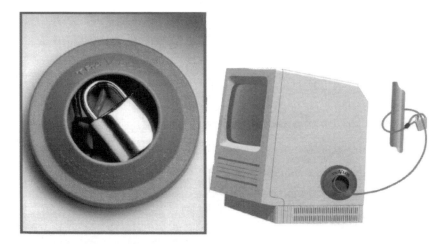

Figure 4–5: Lid locks defend against the theft of internal components.
Reprinted with permission from SecurTech Company.

Marking Your Hardware with Digital Stamps

MICRO-ID is a program that places a digital "stamp" of ownership on IBM compatibles that can later be read by law enforcement personnel with a program called COP-ONLY. An individual user's version of MICRO-ID is included on the CD-ROM that accompanies this book. Look in the MISC directory for the file named *MICRO_ID.ZIP.*

Another product that can help establish ownership when stolen items are recovered is a UV marking pen. The pen leaves an invisible mark on your equipment, which can later be read by a UV light. The pen is available from Innovative Security Products and can be used to mark plastic, metal, wood, paper, glass, and cloth. Innovative Security Products' address can be found at the end of this chapter.

Figure 4–6: The Protect-All Alarm system sets off an alarm when motion is detected.
Reprinted with permission from Innovative Security Products.

replaced with an alarm unit. Both ends of the steel cable are fastened to the alarm unit. If the cable is cut or the alarm is tampered with, the alarm sounds. A separate motion detector switch can be turned off, but if the cable is cut, the alarm will still sound.

LAPTOP SECURITY

Portable computers are easier to carry off than regular-sized PCs, so they present a special security problem. Designers have come up with different systems for fitting portables with alarm systems and physical restraining systems. In this section, I introduce you to four of these systems.

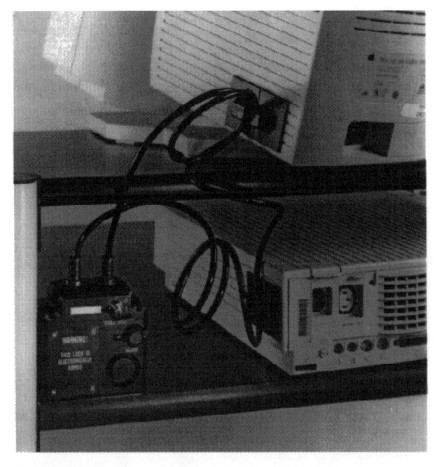

Figure 4–7: Cable and lock security system that attaches to a motion detection device.
Reprinted with permission from Innovative Security Products.

Cable and Anchor

The system shown in Figure 4–8 uses cables and anchor plates much like the systems described earlier for PCs. This system works well when you're traveling with the laptop or working in your office.

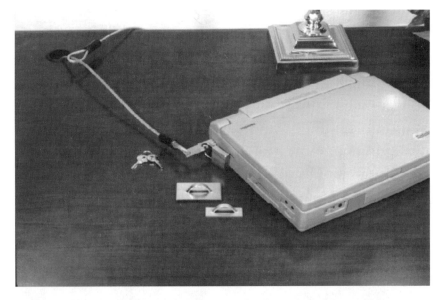

Figure 4–8: Basic lock-down system for portables using a cable, security slot, and padlock.
Reprinted with permission from Innovative Security Products.

The Perrylok Anchor offered by SecurTech, shown in Figure 4–9, operates on a similar principle. However, as with other SecurTech products, the cable and anchor system is self-contained. The Perrylok contains a hand-retractable 14–inch coated steel cable.

Entrapment Device

A second device called an *entrapment*, which is used for securing tower PCs and desktop PCs, can also be used for portables as well. This system works only if the portable computer is intended to remain stationary, however.

Figure 4–9: Perrylok Anchor is a low-profile anchor for securing laptops. The Perrylok attaches to the bottom or back of your laptop case.
Reprinted with permission from SecurTech Company.

Alarm System

The third system available for securing portable computers is an alarm system. You could use an alarm system like the one shown in Figure 4–6, or you could use a device similar to the Alarm Guard by Innovative Security Products. The Alarm Guard consists of two components: a transmitter that you attach to your portable computer and a receiver that you fasten to your belt or place in your pocket. In Figure 4–10, the larger component is the receiver and the smaller component is the transmitter that attaches

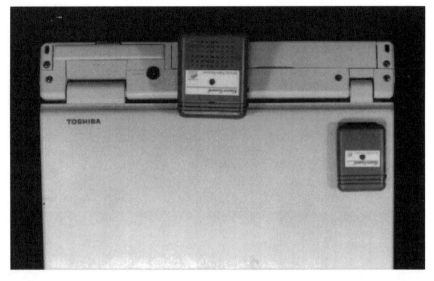

Figure 4–10: An Alarm Guard system including a receiver (left) and transmitter (right) attached to top of laptop.
Reprinted with permission from Innovative Security Products.

to the computer. When the portable computer is moved away from you 15 feet or more (distance depends on location and range setting), a beeping sound notifies you. If a thief turns the transmitter off, the beep sounds continuously.

Drive Locks and Mouse Vandalism

If you cannot attach a lock-down plate to your portable PC, you might consider using a drive lock. A drive lock attaches to the 3.5–inch floppy drive that is built into most notebook and laptop computers. The device is inserted into the floppy disk drive and then twisted and locked. A cable extends from the drive lock to a stationary object such as a table leg.

Another type of drive lock is used to prevent individuals from accessing 3.5–inch PC floppy drives. Innovative Security Products offers the Secure Drive Lock, shown in Figure 4–11. There are two reasons you might consider using a floppy drive lock: It can prevent someone from uploading a virus from an infected floppy disk, and it can prevent someone from downloading important files to a floppy disk.

The Righton Mouseals shown in Figure 4–12 can be used to deter students from removing mouse balls. Mouseals conceal the access disk that when turned and removed, releases the ball. Mouseals also carry a strong warning message: Do Not Remove. SecurTech offers two models: Mylar and Vinyl. Vinyl Mouseals are best if the mouse has a raised surface, and Mylar works well on the newer mice that have flat surfaces around the access disk.

Figure 4–11: Secure Drive Lock prevents access to the 3.5–inch floppy drive.
Reprinted with permission from Innovative Security Products.

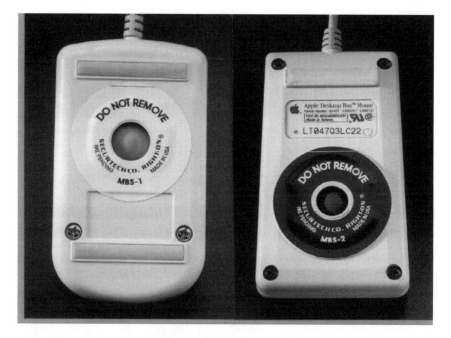

Figure 4–12: Mylar and Vinyl Mouseals help to deter students from tampering with mice.
Reprinted with permission from SecurTech Company.

Insuring against Theft, Viruses, and Breakdowns

Your organization probably has some form of Liability, Building, and Personal Property coverage. Ordinarily there are three forms used for Building and Personal property: (1)Basic, which names specific hazards such as fire and wind; (2)Broad, which adds a few more types of coverage beyond Basic; and (3) Special, which doesn't name specifics, but rather covers everything unless it is specifically excluded. Special Form picks up theft. To make sure that your hardware is protected against theft, ask your insurance agent whether you have Special Form.

Another issue to consider is insuring your system against viruses, Trojan Horses, and mechanical breakdowns. Ordinarily, these aren't covered by the Special Form, but they are covered by a floater called an EDP or TIS form. EDB (Electronic Data Processing Form) is an older form and TIS (Technology Information Systems Form) is a newer form that is replacing the EDB forms. Other insurers may refer to this as a Computer Property Floater.

Building and property are covered under the property section of insurance. Computer software and hardware are covered under an Inland Marine form, which covers items that are movable.

Table 4–1: Sources of hardware security products

Company Name	Address
Anchor Pad International	35 Hammond Irvine, CA 92718 Tele: 714–580–2555, 800–626–2467 FAX: 714–580–2560
Brady Office Machine Security Inc.	11056 S. Bell Ave. Chicago, IL 60643 Tele: 312–779–8349, 800–326–8349 FAX: 312–779–9712
Compu-Guard, Inc.	36 Maple Ave. Seekonk, MA 02771 Tele: 508–761–4520, 800–333–6810 FAX: 508–761–4440
Computer Security Products	One Computer Dr., P.O. Box 204 Northboro, MA 10532 Tele: 508–393–9814, 800–466–7636 FAX: 508–393–2296
Innovative Security Products	P.O. Box 8682 Prairie Village, KS 66208 Tele: 913–385–2002 FAX: 913–642–9546 Web: www.wesecure.com
PC Guardian Security Products	1133 Francisco Blvd. E, Ste. D San Rafael, CA 94901 Tele: 415–459–0190, 800–288–8126 FAX: 415–459–1162
SecurTech Company	5755 Willow Lane Lake Oswego, OR 97035–5340 Tele: 800–800–9573 FAX: 503–636–9642

Chapter 5

Front-End Security for MS-DOS and Windows

Before I built a wall I'd ask to know
What I was walling in or walling out,
And to whom I was like to give offence.
—Robert Frost
(from *North of Boston "Mending Wall"*)

Most schools and libraries with networked PCs employ system administrators to enforce security measures. As a minimum requirement, students and staff are asked to log onto the network with a valid ID and password at boot-up. Some systems then present you with a secure menu system. For added security, system administrators ask students and staff to store their data files in the home directories that have been assigned to them on the network servers instead of their local hard drives.

Servers on networks are usually not the target of amateur hackers because these computers are kept out of public view and relatively secure. If a hacker, other than an insider, were to attempt breaking into a network server, he/she would do it via a local or wide area network. The attack scenario used for accomplishing this would be more advanced than what is typically used to break into a standalone PC. It is an attack your average newbie hacker wouldn't be capable of pulling off.

For this reason, I believe public access computers—the *standalones*—are the preferred "newbie" hacker target. A typical standalone PC that offers Internet access, word processing, CD-ROM database searching, etc., is easy to get to physically and in most cases, unsecured. An inexperienced hacker can quickly gain access to the operating system and add, delete, or write to files.

Chapter 5 addresses this security concern by introducing various front-end security tools that protect programs and data from attacks by unauthorized users. I describe DOS- and Windows-based menu systems; I explain how to restrict access to MS-DOS, Windows 3.x, and Windows 95 operating systems; and I describe a unique hardware/software solution that prevents hackers from permanently writing any programs or data to your hard drive.

SECURING YOUR WINDOWS 3.X COMPUTERS

One of Microsoft's goals has always been to provide a Windows operating environment that is user friendly. Systems that are easy to set up and use present a special problem for system administrators managing public access PCs. The user friendly features make it difficult to maintain security and to keep program and desktop settings consistent day-to-day—sometimes hour-to-hour.

Librarians and lab instructors have tried different approaches for dealing with inadvertent alterations to Program Manager, and malicious attacks by hackers who have the know-how to change program settings and gain unauthorized access to files and data. Systems without password protection were hopelessly vulnerable to attacks. Systems with lots of locks installed on the front door took a long time to get open, were time consuming to maintain, and ended up being less accessible and useable.

The best defense seems to be a user-friendly menu system and minimal restrictions that defend against inadvertent modifications to program settings.

WHAT SHOULD YOU LOOK FOR IN A MENU SYSTEM?

There are a number of menuing systems on the market. Some are very basic, shareware products written for MS-DOS, and others are commercial Windows 95 applications that incorporate advanced graphics and security capabilities. In the sections that follow I show you how to use batch files and a DOS-based menu system to help create a secure Windows 3.x and DOS operating environment. I also introduce you to two Windows-based menu systems: Everybody's Menu Builder and WinU.

Depending on your preferences and the needs of your particular organization, one menu system may work better for you than another. No matter which system you decide to go with, here are some features to consider when making your choice:

- If your system is networked, the PC should force a

user to log onto the LAN and go though the password check.

- Does it prevent a user from unauthorized access to the C: drive?
- Does it disable booting from floppy drives?
- On networked systems, does it make the default storage of files and data to a secure server? (In a setting where staff are working through secure menuing systems, this option helps minimize the chances of storing sensitive information to a floppy disk or local hard disk.)
- Does the menuing system lock the PC after a predetermined period of inactivity? (This is important on networks where the PC forces a user to log onto the LAN and go through a password check.)
- Is there a screen blanking feature that goes along with the inactivity lock?
- Does the menu system maintain usage statistics?
- Does the menu system allow you to run more than one application at a time? Many times it is advantageous to run a word processor at the same time you are searching full text databases. This enables you to cut-and-paste from one application to another.

RUNNING WINDOWS 3.X IN A SECURE ENVIRONMENT

When you use a menu system to run applications in Windows 3.x, many times users gain access to Program Manager after closing out the application. In these instances, mischievous individuals can delete program icons and program groups, or run any program they wish.

> ## Where Has All the Memory Gone?
>
> One of the biggest problems you face when running DOS menu systems is that they do not always leave the system with enough conventional memory to run DOS-based CD-ROM products, such as SIRS, or Academic Abstracts. The problem is compounded when you also try to run a memory resident anti-virus program. There isn't an easy solution to this problem and you may be forced to choose between either a secure menu system or a memory resident anti-virus software. In the past I have opted for the secure menu systems and installed floppy drive locks to protect against viruses being transferred through floppy disks. The long term solution is to plan for a system that operates in a Windows-based environment.

In this section I explain how to restrict access to the Windows operating system when using a DOS-based menuing system called Direct Access. You may find that after thorough testing, the same principles can be applied to other DOS-based menu systems.

SECURING WINDOWS APPLICATIONS

The program that opens when you run Windows and governs how Windows operates is called the *shell program*. Customarily, this is Program Manager in Windows 3.x. It is represented by the *PROGMAN.EXE* file found in the Windows directory. There is a line of text in a file named *SYSTEM.INI*—also located in the Windows directory—that determines which program opens as the shell program.

Figure 5–1 illustrates the [boot] section of a typical *SYSTEM.INI* file. Look for the line that reads, **shell=\windows\progman.exe.**

```
[boot]
mouse.drv=mouse.drv
shell=\windows\progman.exe
network.drv=
language.dll=
sound.drv=mmsound.drv
comm.drv=comm.drv
keyboard.drv=keyboard.drv
system.drv=system.drv
386grabber=VGA.3GR
oemfonts.fon=vgaoem.fon
286grabber=VGACOLOR.2GR
fixedfon.fon=vgafix.fon
fonts.fon=vgasys.fon
display.drv=TRIT640.DRV
drivers=mmsystem.dll
SCRNSAVE.EXE=(None)
```

Figure 5–1: The [boot] section of a *SYSTEM.INI* file

If you wanted to set up a public access PC to run a single application in Windows, you would simply change the designated shell program in *SYSTEM.INI* from *PROGMAN.EXE* to the new program you want to run. (Remember to make a backup copy of the original *SYSTEM.INI* before making any permanent changes like this.) If, for example, you wanted Windows to open to

Notepad, you would change the **shell** statement of the [boot] section to read:

shell=\windows\notepad.exe

When you run Windows with this shell statement, it automatically opens to Notepad. No other programs can be accessed. When you close out Notepad, Windows closes automatically.

> **Changing the Shell Statement in Windows 95.**
> Some individuals find it advantageous to change the shell=explorer.exe line in the Windows 95 *SYSTEM.INI* to shell=progman.exe. This loads Program Manager instead of Windows Explorer for the shell. Program Manager offers less features than Explorer and therefor is less of a security concern.

If you want to have several different menu choices that run various applications in this secure environment, and retain the ability to run a normal Windows session, too, you need to keep a separate *SYSTEM.INI* file for each shell program. The process for accomplishing this is explained next.

How to Run Notepad in a Secure Setting

In this exercise I show you how to set up access to one Windows application called Notepad. There are two methods for accomplishing this. First I show you how to do it using two different *SYSTEM.INI* files: the original *SYSTEM.INI* and one that has the **shell** statement changed to load *NOTEPAD.EXE*. In this first method, the original *SYSTEM.INI* file is temporarily replaced by the revised *SYSTEM.INI* file.

The second method uses a special program named *INI.EXE* which is designed to go into the *SYSTEM.INI* file and rewrite the **shell** statement. In this method, only one *SYSTEM.INI* files exists—the original.

You can repeat either process as many times as you wish to run any number of single applications from the Direct Access menu system.

Method One for Running a Single Application

Here are the steps for running Notepad using the first method described earlier. The original *SYSTEM.INI* file is used for normal Windows operations and a second revised *SYSTEM.INI* is created for running *NOTEPAD.EXE* in a restricted mode.

STEP 1: BACKUP IMPORTANT FILES

Make a backup copy of the *SYSTEM.INI* file found in the Windows directory. You can do this by copying it to another file, such as *SYSTEM.BKP*. Use the **copy** command like this:

    C:\WINDOWS>copy system.ini system.bkp

STEP 2: CREATE A DIRECTORY FOR STORING BATCH FILES

You create a special batch file for every program you wish to run and you store those files in a directory. In this exercise I name the directory BATCH. The command for creating a directory named BATCH is: C:\md BATCH

Step 3: Create a New *SYSTEM.INI* File

Copy the *SYSTEM.INI* file to another file in the BATCH directory and name it something else, such as *SYSTEM.PAD*. The command for accomplishing this is: C:\copy c:\windows\system.ini c:\batch\system.pad

Step 4: Rewrite the Shell Statement

Use a text editor to open the *SYSTEM.PAD* file and change the shell statement to read: **shell=\windows\notepad.exe**

Step 5: Write a Batch File to Invoke Notepad

The menu choice in Direct Access doesn't link directly to *NOTEPAD.EXE*. Instead, it links to a batch file that does three things before returning to the menu system: 1) it copies the original *SYSTEM.INI* file to the BATCH directory and copies the *SYSTEM.PAD* file to the WINDOWS directory; 2) it loads Windows which now opens to Notepad; and 3) it puts the original *SYSTEM.INI* file back into the WINDOWS directory when you close Notepad. Figure 5–2 illustrates how this batch file should be written. I've named it *NOTEPAD.BAT*.

Step 6: Creating the Menu Item

The last step is to create a menu Item in Direct Access that runs Notepad. At the main screen select **F2 Maintenance** and then select **CREATE/MODIFY MAIN MENU**. Next, enter Notepad as a menu item, and then press F9 to create the sub-menu as shown in Figure 5–3. Save your settings and test your work.

```
REM BATCH FILE TO EXECUTE WINDOWS
NOTEPAD AND
REM RETURN TO DIRECT ACCESS MENU.
@echo off
cls
copy c:\windows\SYSTEM.INI c:\batch\system.old
copy c:\batch\system.pad c:\windows\SYSTEM.INI
cd\windows
win
REM PUT THE ORIGINAL SYSTEM.INI FILE BACK IN
PLACE
cd\batch
copy c:\batch\system.old c:\windows\SYSTEM.INI
cd\
```

Figure 5–2: The batch file named NOTEPAD.BAT

Method Two for Running a Single Application

Here are the steps for running Notepad using the second method described earlier. As with the first method, this method uses the original *SYSTEM.INI* file for normal Windows operations. Instead of creating a separate *SYSTEM.INI* file for running *NOTEPAD.EXE*, this method uses a program named *INI.EXE* to go in and rewrite the **shell** statement in the original *SYSTEM.INI* file so it boots up to Notepad instead of Program Manager. If you want to load another program, say Lotus 1–2–3, then you use *INI.EXE* to go in and rewrite the **shell** statement to read something like

   shell=\123r5w\programs\123w.exe

```
        C R E A T E  /  M O D I F Y  S U B - M E N U S
        The Title of This Sub Menu is 'Notepad'.   (2nd Level)

  Program      Description     Drive      Directory      Filename
  -------      -----------     ------     ---------      --------

  A) Notepad                   C:\BATCH                  BATCH NOTEPAD
  B)
  C)
  D)
  E)
  F)
  G)
  H)
  I)
  J)
  K)
  L)
  M)

  F2 Insert                                              F1  Help
  F3 Delete    F5 Custom   F7 Tree   F8 Options  F9 Sub-Menu   Esc Exit
  F4 Move                                                F10 Main
```

Figure 5–3: In Direct Access, file naming conventions require that NOTEPAD.BAT be referenced as BATCH NOTEPAD.

STEP 1: GET A COPY OF *INI.EXE*

You can use one of the FTP search engines on the Web to locate a copy of *INI.EXE* on the Internet, such as FTP search V3.x (*ftpsearch.ntnu.no/ftpsearch*), or go directly to FTP site *ftp.studenti.to.it* and download a copy of *INI.EXE* located in the */pub/policasa/install/util/* directory. If you are accessing this file from the Web, type the following URL in the location box:

ftp://ftp.studenti.to.it/pub/policasa/install/util/INI.EXE

As in the first method, create a directory named BATCH. Now copy *INI.EXE* into the BATCH directory you've just created.

STEP 2: BACKUP IMPORTANT FILES

Make a backup copy of the *SYSTEM.INI* file found in the Windows directory. You can do this by copying it to another file, such as *SYSTEM.BKP*. Use the **copy** command like this:

C:\WINDOWS>copy *SYSTEM.INI* system.bkp

STEP 3: WRITE A BATCH FILE TO INVOKE NOTEPAD

As explained earlier in method one, the menu system doesn't directly link to *NOTEPAD.EXE*. Instead, it links to a batch file that links to Notepad. In this method, however, the batch file is much simpler. Instead of including command lines that trade out the original *SYSTEM.INI* with rewritten versions, this batch file runs *INI.EXE* and instructs it to rewrite the **shell** statement in the original *SYSTEM.INI*. Figure 5–4 illustrates how this batch file should be written. I've named it *NOTEPAD.BAT*.

STEP 4: CREATING THE MENU ITEM

The last step is to create a menu Item in Direct Access that runs Notepad. Follow the same procedures explained in method one, Step 6. Save your settings and test your work.

Running Two Windows Applications Securely at the Same Time

A different process is used to run two applications concurrently while keeping your system secure. This requires manipulating the *PROGMAN.INI* file and Program

```
REM BATCH FILE TO EXECUTE WINDOWS
NOTEPAD AND
REM RETURN TO DIRECT ACCESS MENU.
REM THE INI.EXE PROGRAM SETS THE SHELL STATE-
MENT TO
REM SHELL=\WINDOWS\NOTEPAD.EXE BEFORE
EXECUTING WIN AND
REM SETS IT BACK TO
SHELL=\WINDOWS\PROGMAN.EXE AFTER
REM EXECUTING.
@echo off
CLS
CD\BATCH
ini c:\windows\SYSTEM.INI boot shell
c:\windows\notepad.exe
cd\windows
win
REM REWRITE THE SYSTEM.INI FILE SO IT'S BACK IN
ITS ORIGINAL
REM FORM
cd\batch
ini c:\windows\SYSTEM.INI boot shell
c:\windows\progman.exe
CD\
```

Figure 5–4: The batch file running INI.EXE named NOTEPAD.BAT

Groups. To demonstrate this procedure I use Trumpet Winsock and Netscape Navigator as examples. These two programs work hand-in-hand on a Windows 3.x computer connected to the Internet. Netscape Navigator cannot run without Trumpet Winsock also running in the background.

STEP 1: BACKUP IMPORTANT FILES

Before you begin, create a directory called WINBKUP and copy all of the *.ini and *.grp files to this directory. The commands are:

C:\md WINBKUP	This creates a directory named WINBKUP
C:\copy *.ini c:\WINBKUP	This copies all of the files ending in .ini located in the WINDOWS directory to the WINBKUP directory.
C:\copy *.grp c:\WINBKUP	This copies all of the files ending in .grp to the WINBKUP directory. These represent your program groups.

Each time programs are added to or deleted from your system, make new backup copies of all *.ini and *.grp files.

STEP 2: CREATE A NEW STARTUP GROUP

Start up Windows as you normally would. Once you are in Program Manager, open the Startup group and delete any icons that might be present in that program group. To do this, highlight the icon, hit the delete key, and then confirm the deletion by clicking on the **Yes** button. Repeat this process for every program in this group. Next, enter the programs that you want to run in Startup. In this example that would be Netscape Navigator and Trumpet Winsock. The simplest way to add these two programs to the Startup Group is by clicking and dragging the respective icons into the Startup Group window.

Now copy the *STARTUP.GRP* file to your BATCH directory and rename it something like *STARTUP.NEW*. You can perform this operation in DOS using the following command:

C:\copy c:\windows\startup.grp c:\batch\startup.new

STEP 3: REMOVE REMAINING PROGRAM GROUPS

Your ultimate goal is to have a secure environment with only Netscape and Trumpet Winsock running. To accomplish this, begin by deleting all of the program groups except the Startup Group. This is done by first deleting all of the icons in a single program group. To do this, highlight an icon, hit the delete key, and then confirm the deletion.

Repeat this process for every program in the group. Lastly, delete the program group window itself. Continue this process until all of the program groups are deleted except for the Startup Group.

Now remove the icons from the Startup Group, but leave the Startup Group window remaining. Exit Program Manager and save changes. To save changes when you exit, make sure that option is checked under the **Options** pull down menu.

STEP 4: RESTRICTING AND PROTECTING PROGRAM MANAGER

The *PROGMAN.INI* file makes it possible to set access restrictions that prevent inadvertent changes to your public PCs. Append a new section to your *PROGMAN.INI* file named [Restrictions] and include the appropriate variables shown in Table 5–1.

Using a text editor to edit *PROGMAN.INI*, add the section shown in Figure 5–5 to the end of the file and save the file to the BATCH directory naming it something like *PROGMAN.NEW*.

Avoiding Detection

To make *.ini* files more secure, change their attributes to hidden and read-only. You can do this at the DOS prompt. Go to the directory in which the file is located and type this command: **attrib <filename> +h +r**

For example, to make the *PROGMAN.INI* file, which is located in the C:\WINDOWS directory, hidden and read-only, you would enter: C:\WINDOWS>**attrib PROGMAN.INI +h +r**

To be on the safe side, you may also decide to apply these attributes to the *autoexec.bat, config.sys, command.com,* and *wina20.386* files located in the root directory.

Table 5–1: Variables used in the [Restrictions] section of *PROGMAN.INI*

Variable	Effect
NoClose=1	This disables the **Exit** option from the **File** menu and disables the **ALT-F4** key combination to exit Windows.
NoSaveSettings=1	This disables the **Save Settings on Exit** option from the **Options** menu.
NoRun=1	This disables the **Run** option from the **File** menu. (This prevents users from running programs other than those on the Desktop. It's included in the NoFileMenu variable.)
NoFileMenu=1	This disables the **File** menu altogether.
EditLevel=4	This prevents users from creating, renaming, moving, or deleting groups and items within groups. Also, it prevents users from editing any information in the **Program Item Properties** dialog box which is accessed through the File menu by clicking on **Properties**.

```
[Restrictions]
EditLevel=4
NoSaveSettings=1
NoFileMenu=1
NoClose=1
```

Figure 5–5: Add this section to your PROGMAN.INI file.

Warning

Remember to remove the read-only attribute before you install new software since the installation process will undoubtedly write new information to the *win.ini* and *SYSTEM.INI* files. To remove the hidden and read-only attributes, enter the command **attrib <filename> -h -r**

STEP 5: COPY THE ORIGINAL *PROGMAN.INI* FILE AND *STARTUP.GRP* FILE FROM WINBKUP DIRECTORY TO WINDOWS DIRECTORY.

STEP 6: WRITE A BATCH FILE TO INVOKE NETSCAPE AND TRUMPET WINSOCK

The next step is to write a batch file like the one shown in Figure 5–6. Name it something like *INTERNET.BAT*. The lines beginning with **REM** are remarks that explain what is happening. They are not processed as part of the batch file.

So far, this is what we've done: Created a BATCH directory and in it we've placed a *PROGMAN.INI* file (named *PROGMAN.NEW*) with lots of restrictions; a

```
@ECHO OFF
CLS
CD\BATCH
REM Copies the original PROGMAN.INI file and
STARTUP.GRP REM file in the WINDOWS directory to the
BATCH directory and REM in the process, renames them to
PROGMAN.WIN and
REM STARTUP.WIN
COPY C:\WINDOWS\STARTUP.GRP
C:\BATCH\STARTUP.WIN
COPY C:\WINDOWS\PROGMAN.INI
C:\BATCH\PROGMAN.WIN
REM Copies PROGMAN.NEW and STARTUP.NEW in the
BATCH
REM directory to the WINDOWS directory, renaming them
in the REM process to PROGMAN.INI and STARTUP.GRP
COPY C:\BATCH\STARTUP.NEW
C:\WINDOWS\STARTUP.GRP
COPY C:\BATCH\PROGMAN.NEW
C:\WINDOWS\PROGMAN.INI
REM Starts Windows
CD\WINDOWS
WIN
CD\BATCH
REM Puts the normal PROGMAN.INI file back for normal
Windows
REM and puts the STARTUP group back like it was
COPY C:\BATCH\PROGMAN.WIN
C:\WINDOWS\PROGMAN.INI
COPY C:\BATCH\STARTUP.WIN
C:\WINDOWS\STARTUP.GRP
CD\
```

Figure 5–6: Batch file to execute Tcpman and Netscape

STARTUP group that contains only Tcpman and Netscape; and a batch file named *INTERNET.BAT*. The WINDOWS directory should have the original *.INI and *.GRP files. The last step is to add a menu item to your menu program that runs the *INTERNET.BAT* file.

STEP 7: CREATING THE MENU ITEM

The last step is to create a menu Item in Direct Access that runs Tcpman and Netscape. At the main screen select **F2 Maintenance** and then select **CREATE/MODIFY MAIN MENU**. Next, enter the term "Internet" or "Netscape" as a menu item. Next, press F9 to create the sub-menu as shown in Figure 5–7. Save your settings and test your work.

Added Protection When Rebooting Occurs

If a PC is rebooted while running one of the Windows applications, somehow you have to make sure it reverts back to the original *SYSTEM.INI* and *PROGMAN.INI* files. To insure that this happens, add the text shown in Figure 5–8 to your *AUTOEXEC.BAT* file. Insert it just before the last line in the file which presumably loads your menu system.

OTHER MEANS OF LOCKING DOWN WINDOWS AND DOS

So far in this book I have explained the importance of creating an emergency startup disk (see Chapter 1); how to set CMOS passwords (see Chapter 3); how to insert re-

```
            C R E A T E  /  M O D I F Y  S U B - M E N U S
         The Title of This Sub Menu is 'Notepad'.    (2nd Level)

  Program       Description      Drive         Directory      Filename
  -------       -----------      ------        ---------      ----------

  A)  Notepad                    C:\BATCH                     BATCH NOTEPAD
  B)  Internet                   C:\BATCH                     BATCH INTERNET_
  C)
  D)
  E)
  F)
  G)
  H)
  I)
  J)
  K)
  L)
  M)

  F2 Insert                                                   F1   Help
  F3 Delete      F5 Custom   F7 Tree    F8 Options  F9 Sub-Menu Esc  Exit
  F4 Move                                                     F10  Main
```

Figure 5–7: In the Direct Access menu system, you refer to the INTERNET.BAT file as BATCH INTERNET.

```
REM RESETS SYSTEM FOR NORMAL WINDOWS IN
INSTANCES WHERE PC REM IS REBOOTED WHILE
RESTRICTED
del c:\windows\SYSTEM.INI
copy c:\winbkup\SYSTEM.INI c:\windows\SYSTEM.INI
C:\batch\ini C:\windows\SYSTEM.INI boot shell
progman.exe
COPY C:\BATCH\PROGMAN.WIN
C:\WINDOWS\PROGMAN.INI
COPY C:\BATCH\STARTUP.WIN
C:\WINDOWS\STARTUP.GRP
```

Figure 5–8: View of AUTOEXEC.BAT file showing commands for restoring original Windows system files

strictions in the *PROGMAN.INI* file and delete critical files for security reasons (Chapter 5); and how to make files harder to find and alter by making them hidden and read-only (Chapters 3 and 5). In this section I expand on these ideas and explore other low-budget methods of locking down Windows and DOS.

Introduction to DOS Switches

If you are having problems booting up your PC and you think the problem might exist in your CONFIG.SYS or AUTOEXEC.BAT file, you can bypass all of the commands contained in these files by pressing F5 after starting your computer and seeing the text, "Starting MS-DOS . . . ".

To bypass individual commands contained in the CONFIG.SYS and AUTOEXEC.BAT files, press the F8 key instead of F5. After doing this, MS-DOS reads one line at a time in the CONFIG.SYS and AUTOEXEC.BAT files. After each line, MS-DOS asks you if you want to carry out or bypass the command.

Naturally, hackers also use the F8 and F5 keys to halt the boot process before a secure menu system or anti-virus program loads.

The **switches** command in MS-DOS allows you to implement special options in the CONFIG.SYS file. The /N switch makes it more difficult for users to break into your PC at bootup by disabling the F5 and F8 keys. The /F switch skips the two second delay that comes after the "Starting MS-DOS . . . " message appears. The command **SWITCHES=/N/F** can be added to the first line of the *config.sys* file.

This doesn't disable a hacker from using CTRL+F5 or

CTRL+F8 to keep *DRVSPACE.BIN* from loading. (*DRVSPACE.BIN* provides access to compressed drives compressed using DriveSpace. If you bypass *DRVSPACE.BIN*, you won't be able to get to your DriveSpace compressed drives.) To prevent this from happening, use the **DRVSPACE /SWITCHES** command to add the **SWITCHES /N** command to your *DRVSPACE.INI* file. You must edit the *DRVSPACE.INI* file directly using a text editor such as MS-DOS Editor. The syntax for this command is

DRVSPACE /SWITCHES=N

To learn more about the **SWITCHES** command, refer to a DOS manual or DOS's online help system. You can access online help by entering the **help** command at the DOS prompt.

Configuring Switches for Windows 95

In Windows 95, the *MSDOS.SYS* file contains configuration information that is read during bootup. It doesn't contain much information, but what it does include is very important. The bare bones *MSDOS.SYS* file shown in Figure 5–9 is essentially what you are given when you set up Windows 95.

WHERE CAN YOU FIND THE *MSDOS.SYS* FILE?

The *MSDOS.SYS* file is located in the root directory of your boot drive. It is hidden and read-only, so before you can edit it, remove the read-only attribute. The easiest way to do this is to right-click on the filename in Windows Explorer and then choose Properties. There are check-boxes in the Properties dialog box that enable you to set the attributes on or off.

WHAT DO THE CONFIGURATION SWITCHES MEAN?

The configuration switches in the [**Paths**] section basically tell Windows 95 where to find the boot drive and which directory contains Windows 95. There are over a dozen switches that can be specified in the [**Options**] section.

The **BootGUI=1** switch shown in Figure 5–9 ensures that you boot to Windows. If you would rather boot to DOS

```
[Paths]
UninstallDir=C:\
WinDir=C:\WINDOWS
WinBootDir=C:\WINDOWS
HostWinBootDrv=C

[Options]
BootGUI=1

;
;The following lines are required for compatibility with other programs.
;Do not remove them (MSDOS.SYS needs to be >1024 bytes).
;xxxxxxxxxxxxxxxxxxxxxxxxxxxxxxxxxxxxxxxxxxxxxxxxxxxxxxxxxxxxxxxxa
;xxxxxxxxxxxxxxxxxxxxxxxxxxxxxxxxxxxxxxxxxxxxxxxxxxxxxxxxxxxxxxxxb
;xxxxxxxxxxxxxxxxxxxxxxxxxxxxxxxxxxxxxxxxxxxxxxxxxxxxxxxxxxxxxxxxc
;xxxxxxxxxxxxxxxxxxxxxxxxxxxxxxxxxxxxxxxxxxxxxxxxxxxxxxxxxxxxxxxxd
;xxxxxxxxxxxxxxxxxxxxxxxxxxxxxxxxxxxxxxxxxxxxxxxxxxxxxxxxxxxxxxxxe
;xxxxxxxxxxxxxxxxxxxxxxxxxxxxxxxxxxxxxxxxxxxxxxxxxxxxxxxxxxxxxxxxf
;xxxxxxxxxxxxxxxxxxxxxxxxxxxxxxxxxxxxxxxxxxxxxxxxxxxxxxxxxxxxxxxxg
;xxxxxxxxxxxxxxxxxxxxxxxxxxxxxxxxxxxxxxxxxxxxxxxxxxxxxxxxxxxxxxxxh
;xxxxxxxxxxxxxxxxxxxxxxxxxxxxxxxxxxxxxxxxxxxxxxxxxxxxxxxxxxxxxxxxi
;xxxxxxxxxxxxxxxxxxxxxxxxxxxxxxxxxxxxxxxxxxxxxxxxxxxxxxxxxxxxxxxxj
;xxxxxxxxxxxxxxxxxxxxxxxxxxxxxxxxxxxxxxxxxxxxxxxxxxxxxxxxxxxxxxxxk
;xxxxxxxxxxxxxxxxxxxxxxxxxxxxxxxxxxxxxxxxxxxxxxxxxxxxxxxxxxxxxxxxl
;xxxxxxxxxxxxxxxxxxxxxxxxxxxxxxxxxxxxxxxxxxxxxxxxxxxxxxxxxxxxxxxxm
;xxxxxxxxxxxxxxxxxxxxxxxxxxxxxxxxxxxxxxxxxxxxxxxxxxxxxxxxxxxxxxxxn
;xxxxxxxxxxxxxxxxxxxxxxxxxxxxxxxxxxxxxxxxxxxxxxxxxxxxxxxxxxxxxxxxo
;xxxxxxxxxxxxxxxxxxxxxxxxxxxxxxxxxxxxxxxxxxxxxxxxxxxxxxxxxxxxxxxxp
;xxxxxxxxxxxxxxxxxxxxxxxxxxxxxxxxxxxxxxxxxxxxxxxxxxxxxxxxxxxxxxxxq
;xxxxxxxxxxxxxxxxxxxxxxxxxxxxxxxxxxxxxxxxxxxxxxxxxxxxxxxxxxxxxxxxr
;xxxxxxxxxxxxxxxxxxxxxxxxxxxxxxxxxxxxxxxxxxxxxxxxxxxxxxxxxxxxxxxxs
```

Figure 5–9: The configuration switches contained in the MSDOS.SYS file configure Windows 95 during bootup.

7.0, change the 1 to 0 as in **BootGUI=0**. You can still start Windows by typing **win** at the DOS prompt.

WHICH SWITCH DISABLES THE BREAKOUT KEYS?

If you are having trouble with patrons breaking out of Windows 95 bootup with the F8 or F5 keys, here's how you can disable those keys. Add the **BootKeys=0** to the [**Options**] section of the *MSDOS.SYS* file as shown in Figure 5–10. This will stop most hackers trying to break out of bootup, but not all of them. An easy way around this restriction is to bootup from a floppy disk.

Be sure to reset the file's attributes back to hidden and read-only when you are finished.

The Old "Disappearing Ink" Act

There is a device driver in DOS called *ansi.sys* that controls your keyboard's input and your monitor's output.

You load the device by using the **DEVICE** or **DEVICEHIGH** commands in the *config.sys* file. If you've already added the switches command to the first line of the Windows 3.x *config.sys* file, add this command just below it:

    DEVICE=C:\DOS\ANSI.SYS

Now save *config.sys* and close the file.

Next, open the *autoexec.bat* file and add these two lines to the top of the file: (The first line may already be there.)

    @ECHO OFF
    @ECHO ← [8m

```
[Paths]
UninstallDir=C:\
WinDir=C:\WINDOWS
WinBootDir=C:\WINDOWS
HostWinBootDrv=C

[Options]
BootGUI=1
BootKeys=0


;
;The following lines are required for compatibility with other programs.
;Do not remove them (MSDOS.SYS needs to be >1024 bytes).
;xxxxxxxxxxxxxxxxxxxxxxxxxxxxxxxxxxxxxxxxxxxxxxxxxxxxxxxxxxxxxxxxa
;xxxxxxxxxxxxxxxxxxxxxxxxxxxxxxxxxxxxxxxxxxxxxxxxxxxxxxxxxxxxxxxxb
;xxxxxxxxxxxxxxxxxxxxxxxxxxxxxxxxxxxxxxxxxxxxxxxxxxxxxxxxxxxxxxxxc
;xxxxxxxxxxxxxxxxxxxxxxxxxxxxxxxxxxxxxxxxxxxxxxxxxxxxxxxxxxxxxxxxd
;xxxxxxxxxxxxxxxxxxxxxxxxxxxxxxxxxxxxxxxxxxxxxxxxxxxxxxxxxxxxxxxxe
;xxxxxxxxxxxxxxxxxxxxxxxxxxxxxxxxxxxxxxxxxxxxxxxxxxxxxxxxxxxxxxxxf
;xxxxxxxxxxxxxxxxxxxxxxxxxxxxxxxxxxxxxxxxxxxxxxxxxxxxxxxxxxxxxxxxg
;xxxxxxxxxxxxxxxxxxxxxxxxxxxxxxxxxxxxxxxxxxxxxxxxxxxxxxxxxxxxxxxxh
;xxxxxxxxxxxxxxxxxxxxxxxxxxxxxxxxxxxxxxxxxxxxxxxxxxxxxxxxxxxxxxxxi
;xxxxxxxxxxxxxxxxxxxxxxxxxxxxxxxxxxxxxxxxxxxxxxxxxxxxxxxxxxxxxxxxj
;xxxxxxxxxxxxxxxxxxxxxxxxxxxxxxxxxxxxxxxxxxxxxxxxxxxxxxxxxxxxxxxxk
;xxxxxxxxxxxxxxxxxxxxxxxxxxxxxxxxxxxxxxxxxxxxxxxxxxxxxxxxxxxxxxxxl
;xxxxxxxxxxxxxxxxxxxxxxxxxxxxxxxxxxxxxxxxxxxxxxxxxxxxxxxxxxxxxxxxm
;xxxxxxxxxxxxxxxxxxxxxxxxxxxxxxxxxxxxxxxxxxxxxxxxxxxxxxxxxxxxxxxxn
;xxxxxxxxxxxxxxxxxxxxxxxxxxxxxxxxxxxxxxxxxxxxxxxxxxxxxxxxxxxxxxxxo
;xxxxxxxxxxxxxxxxxxxxxxxxxxxxxxxxxxxxxxxxxxxxxxxxxxxxxxxxxxxxxxxxp
;xxxxxxxxxxxxxxxxxxxxxxxxxxxxxxxxxxxxxxxxxxxxxxxxxxxxxxxxxxxxxxxxq
;xxxxxxxxxxxxxxxxxxxxxxxxxxxxxxxxxxxxxxxxxxxxxxxxxxxxxxxxxxxxxxxxr
;xxxxxxxxxxxxxxxxxxxxxxxxxxxxxxxxxxxxxxxxxxxxxxxxxxxxxxxxxxxxxxxxs
```

Figure 5–10: Adding the BootKeys=0 **to the MSDOS.SYS file**

You create the ← which is the escape character 27, by holding the CTRL key down as you press the **p** followed by the [character.

These changes to the *config.sys* and *autoexec.bat* file make typing characters in DOS an invisible process. It may be disorienting to a hacker who cannot tell which directory he/she is in. Nothing will appear on the screen when the command **dir** is entered. If you choose to remove this feature, you can still open the *autoexec.bat* file and remove the @ECHO ← [8m line. Although you won't see the command **edit autoexec.bat** echo to the screen, it will still work.

BUILT-IN SECURITY FEATURES FOR WINDOWS 95

Windows 95 offers you a couple of different methods for securing standalone workstations. You can implement password protection by using the Password Properties dialog box. This is accessed through Control Panel by double-clicking on the icon labeled **Passwords**. This security feature, however, is just as easy to turn off as it is to turn on. And, as was pointed out in Chapter 3, hackers can delete or rename the *.PWL* files which store the system passwords.

Another tool, called the System Policy Editor, enables you to backup configuration changes with a system policy change. When you go in and make changes, for example, in a password setting, then you use the System Policy Editor to go in right behind it and set restrictions on certain types of access. The System Policy Editor is included on the Windows 95 CD-ROM. You install the System Policy Editor by using the **Add/Remove Programs** option in Control Panel. (In Chapter 7, I introduce a friendly front-end to the System Policy Editor called WinSafe.)

Installing the System Policy Editor

Follow these steps to install the System Policy Editor:

1. Click on **Start|Settings|Control Panel** and then double-click on **Add/Remove Programs**.

2. Select the **Windows Setup** tab and click the **Have Disk** button.
3. Now enter the drive letter for your CD-ROM drive (for example, D:\), followed by the path statement *admin\apptools\poledit*. Click **OK**.
4. Place a check in the box next to **System Policy Editor** and click **Install**.
5. Click **OK** to close the **Add/Remove** dialog box.

Making Backups of Important Files

Before you begin setting restrictions on your desktop, make backups of your important files. Follow these steps:

1. Make a Windows 95 emergency startup disk, according to the instructions presented at the end of Chapter 1.
2. Make backup copies of *user.dat* and *system.dat*, both of which are located in the C:\WINDOWS directory. Windows 95 stores the Registry information in these two hidden, read-only system files. Follow these steps to make those copies:

   • Begin by restarting your PC.
   • When the *Starting Windows 95* message appears, press F8 so your machine boots up in Safe Mode.
   • Choose **Safe Mode Command Prompt Only** from the list of menu options.
   • At the system prompt, go to the C:\WINDOWS directory where the *user.dat* and *system.dat* files are stored and change the files' attributes. To do this, type the following commands at the Safe

Mode command prompt, pressing ENTER after each: **attrib user.dat -s -h -r** and **attrib system.dat -s -h -r.**

- Copy the *user.dat* and *system.dat* files to a floppy disk with these commands, pressing ENTER after each: **copy user.dat a:** and **copy system.dat a:.**

- Restore the original attributes by typing these commands at the system prompt and pressing ENTER after each: **attrib user.dat +s +h +r** and **attrib system.dat +s +h +r.**

3. Now shut your computer off at the power switch and turn it back on.

Setting Restrictions for a Single Workstation

Now that the System Policy Editor is installed and your important files are backed up, you can begin setting restrictions on the Windows 95 desktop. Here are the steps to follow:

1. Open the System Policy Editor by choosing the **Run** command. Click on **Start|Run** and then type **poledit** in the text box and click on **OK.**
2. When the System Policy Editor Window opens, click on the **File** pull-down menu and choose the **Open Registry** option. Two icons appear: Local User and Local Computer.
3. Double-click on the Local User icon.
4. Open the **Shell** folder.
5. Open the **Restrictions** subfolder.

Restoring the Windows 95 Registry

Windows 95 has a built-in safeguard that can help you in the event something goes wrong with the registry during editing. By following the procedures described here, you can restore the registry to the state it was in when you last started your PC. You do this by replacing the *user.dat* and *system.dat* files with two "mirror" files named *user.da0* and *system.da0*. (Note that the "0" in .da0 is the number zero.)

Normally you wouldn't restore the register manually. Windows 95 is programmed to restore the registry automatically as part of system startup. Windows 95 usually gets it right, but if you are concerned that a problem you have created in the registry may get copied to the DAO backups, use the procedure given here to restore manually the registry from the backup files:

- Restart your PC in MS-DOS mode.
- Change to the C:\WINDOWS directory.
- Type these commands at the system prompt and press ENTER after each one:
  Attrib -h -r -s system.dat
  attrib -h -r -s system.da0
  copy system.da0 system.dat
  attrib -h -r -s user.dat
  attrib -h -r -s user.da0
  copy user.da0 user.dat
- Restart your computer.

> **WARNING**
>
> Be sure to read this entire section and the following section, "Changing the Taskbar Properties," before you make any permanent changes and reboot your computer.

Under the **Restrictions** heading (see Figure 5–11) you can choose which restrictions you want to enforce on your Windows 95 PC. To make a selection, click on the check box just to the left of the option titles.

Most of the options shown in Figure 5–11 will close up the biggest security holes and prevent hackers from using the Windows shell to their advantage. Of all the restrictions listed, here are the most reasonable choices to make for a public-access PC:

- Remove the Run command
- Remove folders from Settings on Start menu
- Remove Taskbar from Settings on Start menu
- Remove the Find command
- Hide drives in My Computer
- Hide all items on Desktop
- Do not save settings at exit

Removing the Run command is probably the most valuable restriction in the lot. It prevents hackers from running applications on the hard drive, such as the System Policy Editor and Registry editor. Because choosing to "Hide all items on Desktop" precludes library patrons from accessing any programs on your system, this restriction should be used only if you plan to replace the desktop with a secure menu system.

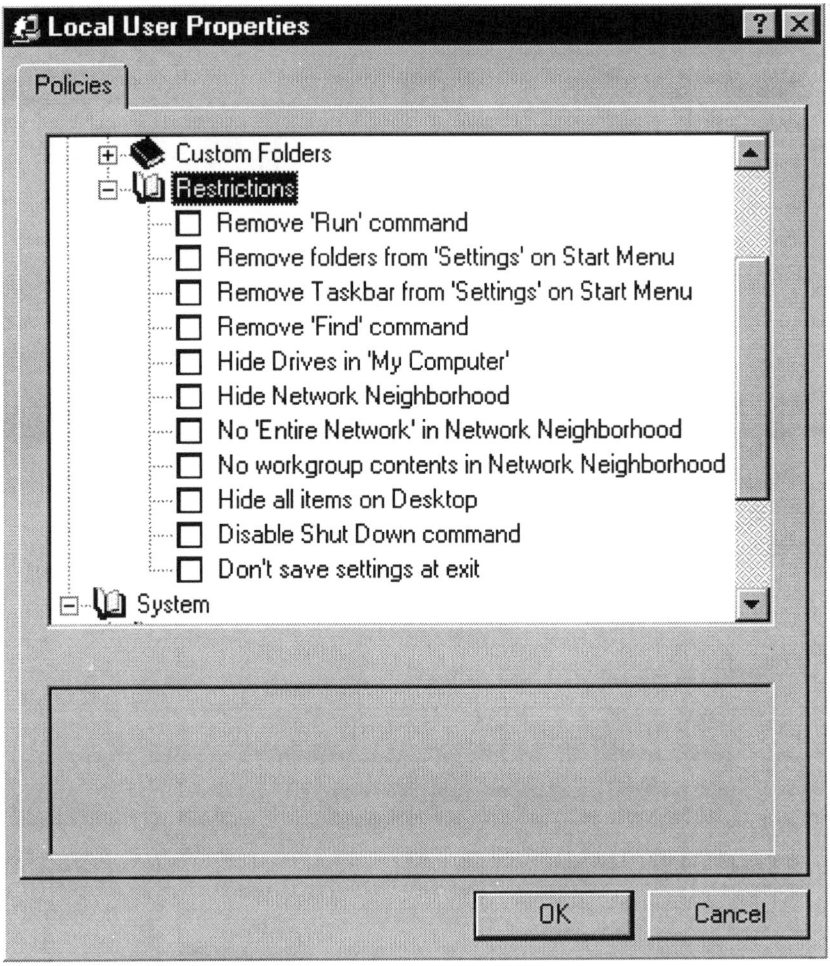

Figure 5–11: The System Policy Editor helps you set restrictions on the Windows 95 desktop.

Another level of restrictions is available under the **System|Restrictions** subheading. Here are two restrictions you can try, depending on your personal preferences:

- Disable Registry editing tools. (Before checking this option, make sure that you test the other options and that you are satisfied with the way they work.)
- Disable the MS-DOS prompt.

Resource Tip

The Windows95 Annoyances home page at *www. creativelement.com/win95ann/* contains a list of annoying "features" of Windows95 and offers solutions for working around most of them.

CHANGING THE TASKBAR PROPERTIES

The changes you made won't take effect until you restart your computer. Before you restart it, however, make the following changes in the **Taskbar Properties** dialog box (get there by clicking on **Start|Settings|Taskbar**):

1. Click on the **Taskbar Options** tab and check the **Auto hide** option. All other options should be unchecked.
2. Click on the **Start Menu Programs** tab and then click on the **Clear** button. This removes the contents of the Documents Menu.
3. Click on the **Remove** button and open the **Programs** folder. Before you proceed any further, decide whether there are any programs you would like patrons to access through the Start menu. If you intend to use a secure menu system, your menu items will provide the means by which patrons access programs,

and there won't be any need to leave programs listed in the Start menu. Secure menu systems ordinarily load from the StartUp folder, so leave that folder and remove all the rest.

4. To remove a folder, highlight the folder's name and then click on **Remove**. When you are finished, click **Close** and then **OK**.

Disabling Access to Find a Folder or File

As with many options in Windows, you can access certain features by either choosing a menu item or by using a function key shortcut. The **Find a Folder or File** option can be activated by pressing F3 even if you removed the menu choice earlier, using the System Policy Editor. You can disable the function associated with the F3 key by assigning a different program to it; for example, the Windows calculator. Here is how it is done:

1. Open Windows Explorer and double-click on the Windows directory name. (If you already instituted the security options discussed earlier and restarted your machine, you won't have access to Windows Explorer via the Start menu, so do this operation before you reboot.)

2. Scroll down until you find the file named *calc.exe*. Highlight it by clicking on it with the left mouse button.

3. Now right-click on *calc.exe* and choose the **Properties** option from the popup menu. (On some systems the file name may appear only as *calc* without the *.exe* extension. In this instance, try clicking on the **View** pull-down menu in Windows Explorer and then clicking on **Details**.)

4. After the **Calculator Properties** box opens, click on the **Shortcut** tab.
5. Now right-click on *calc.exe* and choose the **Create Shortcut** option from the pop-up menu. This should place a file at the bottom of the Windows directory named *Shortcut to Calc.exe*. Right-click on *Shortcut to Calc.exe* and then choose **Cut**. Close Windows Explorer, right-click on your desktop, and choose **Paste**. This action should place the calculator icon on your desktop.
6. Left-click on the calculator icon to highlight it. Now right-click and choose **Properties**.
7. After the Calculator Properties box opens, click on the **Shortcut** tab.
8. Click on **Shortcut key editing**.
9. Press the F3 key and it should replace the word *None* that was previously occupying that box.
10. Click **OK** to save your changes.

Now when hackers press the F3 key thinking they will bring up the **Find: All Files** dialog box, they will instead start the Calculator program running.

WHAT IS EVERYBODY'S MENU BUILDER?

Everybody's Menu Builder Version 2.0 is a secure, Windows-based menu system developed by CARL Corporation. It supports Windows and DOS applications, including Web browsers, CD-ROM products, and Online Public Access Catalogs. It also supports CARL's own products: NoveList, Electric Library, and Kid's Catalog.

Everybody's Menu Builder consists of three main components: Everybody's Menu Builder, Everybody's Menu, and LView.

The Menu Builder, which is associated with the file *menu_bld.exe*, enables you to create your own custom menus. You are given the options to create screen titles, such as **Welcome to our library!**, custom menu items, menu item descriptions, and icons.

Everybody's Menu, which is associated with the file *everybdy.exe*, is the application with which your patrons interact. This menu is the resulting menu you create using Everybody's Menu Builder. Figure 5–12 is a sample menu I created for demonstration purposes. The file *demo.bpf* is a sample menu that comes with the program. Any custom menus you create end with the .bpf extension.

LView is a freeware image editor and viewer developed by Leonardo Loureiro. LView is included with Everybody's Menu Builder to assist you in designing icons for your graphical buttons. You can find three folders in the *e_menu* subdirectory that are filled with dozens of icons you can use to customize your menu screen. Look for the files named *icon1.bmp*, *icon2.bmp*, and *icon3.bmp*.

Which Security Features Are Offered?

Everybody's Menu offers three levels of security.

1. One level is password protection, and this option is set through the **Properties** menu option in Everybody's Menu. This option hides the menu bar and enables you to leave Everybody's Menu and go to DOS or Windows only if you present the correct password. To display the password dialog box while Everybody's Menu is running, press CTRL+Spacebar.

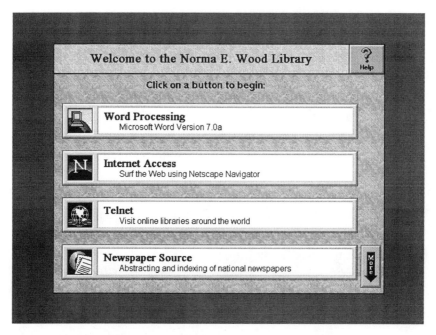

Figure 5–12: Everybody's Menu allows you to create custom icons and menu items in a secure environment.

2. The second level of security loads a virtual device driver file named *nosyskey.386,* which disables certain breakout keys, such as CTRL+ALT+DEL. During installation, you are asked whether you want to activate this Windows keyboard security option. (Additional details on this feature are addressed in Chapter 3.)

3. The third level of security helps protect your system when DOS applications are launched. This is accomplished by creating Program Information Files, or PIFs. The user guide that ships with the Menu Builder's software thoroughly explains how to create PIFs in Windows 3.x and Windows 95.

Adding Everybody's Menu to the StartUp Group

During installation, you are asked whether you would like Everybody's Menu to launch every time you start Windows. If you elect *not* to launch Everybody's Menu every time you start Windows, and then later change your mind, you must then add it manually to the Windows StartUp group. To accomplish this task in Windows 95, click on **Start|Programs|Windows Explorer**. Next, go to the e_menu subdirectory and left-click once on the file named *everybdy.exe*. Once the file name is highlighted, right-click on the file name and then choose **Create Shortcut**. Lastly, cut and paste the *Shortcut to everybdy.exe* file to the Windows/Start Menu/Programs/StartUp folder. Now reboot your machine to test it.

CARL's release of Version 2.0 added several new features, including the ability to password protect individual menu choices, track which applications are being used and for how long, and use a new interface that allows up to 10 menu buttons on a single screen.

Where Can I Get Everybody's Menu Builder?

Orders for Everybody's Menu Builder can be placed online at *www.carl.org/emb/emb.html*, or you can contact CARL Corporation at 3801 East Florida Ave., Suite 300, Denver, Colorado 80210; Phone (303)758–3030; FAX (303)758–0606; e-mail *menu@carl.org*. Pricing is based on a per unit, per year cost. One unit per year costs approximately $39.95 plus $7.95 for shipping and handling.

WINU FROM BARDON DATA SYSTEMS, INC.

WinU has been on the leading edge of Windows 95 menu systems since Version 1.0 was released on August 24, 1995—the same day Windows 95 was released. Now on Version 4.1, WinU continues to be a top-rated secure menu system. (For supporting articles, enter **search** in the URL window at the top of your browser. This connects you to search.com, a service of CNET, Inc. Search on the key words **WinU reviews.**)

Some of WinU's security features include these: you can lock access to any program on your system; password-protect or disable CTRL-ALT-DEL entirely; disable the right-click context menus; and use a new feature called "window control," which enables you to close any window when it appears, such as the Save/Open dialogs. WinU has another feature that tracks when and how long each program on its menu is run and saves this information to a log file.

A new feature that was added to WinU 4.1 is the ability to monitor and log all Web browser activity. WinU tracks which sites are visited and the length of each visit. This information is then made available through WinU reports, or it can be exported to a spreadsheet or database program.

What Are WinU's Three Security Modes?

Depending on your personal preferences, you can set WinU to operate in any one of three different security modes:

1. **No Security "Convenience" Mode**—This mode of operation offers no security at all. The menu screen

helps you organize your favorite applications, but it doesn't lock intruders out.

2. **Casual Security Mode**—Casual Security is the state WinU is in when you first install it. You can run it full screen or smaller than full screen. Your entire system is available in Casual Mode. There are no forced time-outs or restart restrictions.

3. **Super Security Mode**—In the Super Security mode, WinU is the only means through which you can gain access to your system. The Taskbar is gone, shortcuts do not work, there are no desktop icons, and there is no Task Manager. When you close down WinU in Convenience Mode, any applications that were running continue to run. In Super Security Mode, your system shuts down entirely when you exit WinU.

Where Can I Get WinU?

A trial version of WinU is included with the CD-ROM that accompanies this book. Look in the *ACCESS* directory for a file named *BDSWINU.EXE*. You can download the latest version of WinU from Bardon Data Systems' Web site at *www.bardon.com*. A single-user copy of WinU is $49.95. You can also contact Bardon Data Systems, Inc., by writing to them at 1164 Solano Ave. #415, Albany, CA 94706; Phone (510) 526–8470; FAX (510) 526–1271.

COMPARING WINU WITH EVERYBODY'S MENU

I have used both systems extensively and find pluses and minuses in both. One nice feature that WinU offers is that you can use any bitmap image you wish as the background behind your menu buttons. It can be configured so that the image fills the full screen or fills only the top half. You could use an image of your school, business, or library, or an artist's rendering of the new building you are planning. The default image offered by WinU—a bright red and blue WinU logo—isn't too appealing compared to the more polished look of Everybody's Menu.

The large icons and button bars in Everybody's Menu enable you to include not only a title, but also a brief description of the menu item, right on the button. The size, however, limits you to viewing a maximum of 10 buttons (with Version 2.0) on a single screen. To view more, you have to page down. WinU uses a much smaller button image, but you can place many more choices on a single screen.

If you are working in an organization that supports both Windows 3.x and Windows 95 PCs, Everybody's Menu has a distinct advantage. You can run Everybody's Menu on either version of Windows and thus keep your menu system looking consistent throughout your system. WinU, however, runs only on Windows 95 machines.

HARDWARE/SOFTWARE SOLUTION FROM CENTURION TECHNOLOGIES

Centurion Technologies, Inc., offers a unique solution for many of the security problems discussed in this book. Centurion Guard (TM), shown in Figure 5–13, is a hardware-device that electronically write-protects your PC's hard drive. Once you have your system set up the way you want it, you lock Centurion Guard to prevent any further permanent changes to the hard drive. The locking device is mounted in a key-lock plate that you insert in an unused expansion slot in the back of your PC. The system is locked or unlocked by turning a removable key.

How Does Centurion Guard Work?

Centurion Guard protects your system by creating a partition on your hard drive, designated as drive D:, where data is stored temporarily. While Centurion Guard is enabled, any program that attempts to write to the C:\ drive is redirected to the separate, non-write protected area on your hard drive. The Centurion hardware driver loads during bootup and the breakout keys are disabled, so hackers can't break-in easily.

Lock and Load "The Guard"

To illustrate Centurion Guard's effectiveness, imagine this scenario: You have a public-access PC and everyone has unrestricted access to DOS and Windows. Your PC is free of viruses and you have Program Manager set up just the way you like it. You have Centurion Guard installed on the PC, it is locked (enabled), and you open the doors for business.

During the course of the morning, patrons delete icons, hack your Web browser, edit system files with Notepad, and download and run a virus-infected application. You

Figure 5–13: Centurion Guard prevents permanent changes from being made to the hard drive.
Used with permission from Centurion Technologies, Inc.

walk by your PC on your way to lunch and see a screen saver that reads, "HaD bY DaRkFoOl."

To return your PC back to its original state, you simply reboot. Every change that was made while Centurion Guard was enabled is automatically wiped off the hard drive. It is as simple as that. If you want to make any permanent changes yourself, you unlock Centurion Guard with a key, make the changes, and then re-lock the system so it is secure.

Is Centurion Guard the Best Solution?

No security device answers every organization's security needs and Centurion Guard is no exception. Here are a few points to consider when weighing the pros and cons of investing in Centurion Guard:

- Although Centurion Guard prevents viruses from making *permanent* changes to your hard drive, it may not prevent viruses from infecting disks inserted into the floppy drive while viruses are resident in memory. Because it is a concern for most schools and libraries to provide secure environments within which to work, you should consider running anti-virus software in conjunction with Centurion Guard.

- If you are running a secure menu system that tracks usage, this data will not be written permanently to your hard drive while Centurion Guard is enabled. If you rely heavily on usage statistics to support your decisions for adding or removing programs on PCs, or for supporting the purchase of additional public-access PCs, this is an important restriction to consider.

- If you are looking for a complete solution—a PC that's secure and offers a friendly, menu-driven interface—Centurion Guard offers only part of the solution. Although it provides excellent security protection, you are still left with desktop icons as your only means of linking patrons to applications. In this scenario, patrons theoretically could be deleting and moving icons regularly. You would have to monitor your PCs, rebooting them every time someone changes the desktop beyond recognition or changes Netscape's preferences, for example. You may also want to install a secure menu system so your patrons have a display that offers clear choices and remains constant throughout the day.

There are situations, of course, where many of these issues are not a concern. Good examples include classrooms, public computer labs, and learning resource centers, where the preferred interface is Program Manager or the Windows 95 desktop. In these settings, it is paramount for students to have unrestricted access to the system's resources so they can learn how everything works. If students mess up or leave machines in unusable states, rebooting gets everything back to its original state when you are running Centurion Guard. If your organization can support it, you should, in addition to using Centurion Guard, implement a strong anti-virus protection program to help ensure the safest possible environment.

Where Can I Get Centurion Guard?

Centurion Guard sells for $79 per unit to educational institutions. Discounts are offered on quantity purchases. To learn more about Centurion Guard, check out Centurion Technologies, Inc., on the Web at *www.centuriontech.com* or call them at (800)547–5342 or (314)894–2269. You can contact their sales office via e-mail at *sales@ centuriontech.com* or by writing to Centurion Technologies, Inc., 12430 Tesson Ferry Road, Suite 219, St. Louis, MO 63128.

Chapter 6

Protecting against Damage from Viruses

Virii are wondrous creations written for the sole purpose of spreading and destroying the systems of unsuspecting fools.
—from *Dark Angel's Phunky Virus Writing Guide*

Viruses are a threat to anyone operating a personal computer. According to the National Computer Security Association's (NCSA) *1997 Virus Prevalence Survey* (*www.ncsa.com/pressrelease/pr5.html*), 99.33 percent of all medium and large organizations in North America have been hit by at least one computer virus. NCSA estimates that 406 out of every 1,000 computers are infected annually.

The information I present in Chapter 6 will help you understand what viruses are and recognize signs of virus activity before significant damage occurs. This chapter provides you with instructions on how to defend against virus attacks and restore your systems while sustaining minimal losses. This chapter also points out the limitations of anti-virus software so that you will not depend entirely on the claims made by anti-virus software vendors.

WHAT IS A COMPUTER VIRUS?

A *computer virus* is a small computer program that infects your computer applications or system files in computer memory or on disk. In the case of macro viruses, they can also infect data files. Some viruses remain dormant for an undisclosed amount of time, and others become immediately active. An important feature of any virus is that it replicates itself, usually by attaching itself to program files. When activated, viruses can destroy data, delete files, encrypt parts of your hard drive, or display annoying messages on your screen, such as, "Your PC is now stoned! LEGALIZE MARIJUANA!"

WHAT TYPES OF VIRUSES ARE THERE?

Viruses are classified according to the way they infect your computer. *Boot sector viruses* infect the boot sector of floppy disks and the Master Boot Record (MBR) of hard disk drives. *Executable* or *"file" viruses* attack executable program files, such as DOS programs. *Macro viruses* are a new strain of viruses that are becoming very prevalent. These infect data files, most often, Microsoft Word. *Multipartite viruses* are viruses that are a combination of a boot sector virus and a file virus.

Virus Alert Calendar

McAfee maintains a Virus Alert Calendar on their Web site at *www.mcafee.com/support/techdocs/vinfo/act6.asp*. This is a handy tool for keeping up-to-date on viruses that activate on a particular date. For example, during the month of January, McAfee's calendar points out that there are 27 special dates on which viruses may do something other than just infect your PC. The KOMPU.A macro virus can infect your system on any day of any month, but it only activates on certain days. When you open a Word file infected with the KOMPU.A virus on the 6th or 8th day of the month, an InputBox opens which displays the phrase, "Mul on paha tuju! Tahan kommi!" You have to enter **komm** before you can proceed.

Warning

In May 1995, the CIAC (Computer Incident Advisory Capability) issued a warning about a fake version of PKZIP called *PKZ300B.ZIP* or *PKZ300.ZIP*. This is a Trojan program that attempts to delete all the directories on your hard drive. It is extremely rare and was last sighted over a year ago. To be on the safe side, go directly to PKWARE's home page at *www.pkware.com* if you want to get the latest version of PKZIP.

WHAT ARE THE MOST COMMONLY FOUND VIRUSES?

According to the *NCSA 1997 Computer Virus Prevalence Survey*, macro viruses are the most commonly found viruses. They are now two and a half times as common as boot sector viruses. Currently, the most prevalent macro viruses are attacking Microsoft Word 6.0 for Windows, Word 6.0.1 for Macintosh, Word 6.0 for Windows NT, and Word for Windows 95 documents. Other applications besides Windows applications also have the potential of being damaged by macro viruses.

Some of the common boot sector, macro, and multipartite viruses you are likely to find invading your organization include:

- Anti-EXE - Boot sector virus
- Form - Boot sector virus
- Junkie - Multipartite that infects both COM files and Master Boot Record
- Michealangelo - Boot sector virus
- Monkey B - Boot sector virus
- NYB - (New York Boot) Boot sector virus
- Stoned - Boot sector virus
- WM Concept - Macro virus that infects Microsoft Word for Windows documents
- WM.Npad - Macro virus that infects Microsoft Word for Windows documents
- WM Wazzu - Macro virus that infects Microsoft Word for Windows documents

HOW DO VIRUSES USUALLY SPREAD?

Viruses try to increase their odds of survival by making copies of themselves. *Memory resident viruses* replicate by getting into your computer's memory and from there copying themselves to your hard disk or a floppy disk. If a virus copies itself to a floppy disk and you use that disk in another computer, it can spread to that computer's memory.

Non-resident viruses usually do not take up residence in memory. If they do, they leave memory after the host program is closed. This type of virus spreads only when you execute an application that is infected. Sometimes when you run an infected program, the virus does not activate until a later date. When it finally activates, it can severely damage the data stored on your hard drive, or it may simply display a message.

Stealth viruses hide the infection of the hard disks and floppy disks. When the virus is resident in memory or on your hard disk, it "fools" your system, so everything appears to be normal. The best way to discover the existence of a virus that uses stealth is to boot from a clean backup floppy disk and then scan the hard drive. (Details on how to create an emergency backup disk are presented in Chapter 1.)

Polymorphic viruses are challenging to detect because they mutate and look different each time they infect—always trying to hide their true identity. Polymorphic viruses and viruses with stealth qualities spread more easily on PCs that are not protected with up-to-date anti-virus software.

Tip

Virus programs cannot spread in e-mail messages. Although infected programs or data files can be *attached* to e-mail messages, e-mail itself cannot contain a virus program that executes when you read a message. At present, e-mail programs only display messages on your screen; they do not execute programs. To be on the safe side, always scan programs attached to e-mail. Scan Microsoft Word and Excel files for macro viruses.

HOW CAN YOU AVOID INFECTION?

To help prevent the spread of viruses, make your staff aware of these potential sources of infection:

- Floppy disks, including demo programs, floppy disks used by service technicians and LAN supervisors, and floppy disks employees bring from home
- Programs downloaded from online services including BBSs and the Internet
- Files downloaded while browsing the Web
- E-mail attachments (especially Microsoft Word documents)

HOW DO MACRO VIRUSES SPREAD?

Macro viruses are carried in word processing documents and spreadsheets, most commonly Microsoft Word and Excel. *Macros* are instructions carried out by a computer program that can be embedded into data files. For ex-

---

Write-Protecting Your Floppy Disks

A simple way to protect your floppy disks from viruses is to write-protect them. For 5.25–inch disks, cover the write-protect notch with opaque tape. For 3.5–inch floppy disks, slide open the write-protect hole in the corner of the case.

---

ample, you can use macros to add automatically your name, address, and phone number to every document you write instead of doing it manually. Macro viruses latch themselves onto this embedded code found in documents and spreadsheets and travel on networks through e-mail attachments and on floppy disks. Macro viruses are activated by any activities which invoke the infected macros or by opening and closing documents.

CAN VIRUSES CAUSE HARDWARE DAMAGE?

The idea that viruses can cause damage to your system's hardware components is more folklore than fact. Some viruses can make it appear that you have a hardware problem. For example, the Rainbow virus alters your Master Boot Record in such a way that your machine hangs when you try to restart it with a clean, emergency boot disk. This may lead you to think that your hard disk drive is malfunctioning.

Tip
Whenever you download software from the Internet, scan it for viruses before running it.

HOW DO YOU DETECT AND ERADICATE VIRUSES?

You use a special program called *anti-virus software* to find and remove viruses that have infected your system. Anti-virus software fights viruses with a number of tools including signature- and heuristic-based scanning, memory-resident monitoring, and expert detection systems.

Signature- and Heuristic-based Scanning

Signature-based scanning examines every file on the drive you specify. *Signatures* are the fingerprints of computer viruses—the strings of code that are unique to a particular virus. When a scanner identifies a signature match, it can name it and tell you on which drive it is located. When some scanners recognize a virus, they also recommend the best method for removing the virus. If they do not, try consulting an online virus database for advice. Dr. Solomon's Virus Central or McAfee Virus Pages both offer free access to their libraries. (See the end of the chapter for addresses.) You manually can scan a particular file or an entire disk at any time. You can also set your anti-virus software to scan automatically, for example, when you boot up. *Heuristic-based scanners* use operations that might detect an unknown virus.

Memory-Resident Monitoring

Although virus scanners look for viruses only while they are running, *memory-resident monitoring* is a tool that operates in the background while other programs are running. On public-access PCs, this is a convenient tool for real-time, continuous monitoring. The disadvantage of using memory-resident software is that it can use up too much memory and have adverse effects on how other programs run. This is especially true on PCs that run a number of DOS-based applications.

Some of the PCs in my library run DOS-based CD-ROM products that need a minimum of 580KB of free memory and these same PCs were running Direct Access, a DOS-based menu system also loading into conventional memory. When I installed anti-virus software and configured it so the memory-resident software loaded on boot up, we started having problems. When patrons ran one of the CD-ROM products, the program would hang because the anti-virus software and menu system were using too much of the conventional memory. (The DOS operating system can only use the first 640KB of memory.)

The only way to get around this problem is to try and free up some of the conventional memory by moving certain device drivers and memory-resident programs to upper memory. If you have a 80386 or 80486 processor and extended memory, you can try running MemMaker. This is a DOS program that optimizes your computer's memory. You can run MemMaker by first closing Windows and then typing the command **memmaker** at the DOS prompt. If this doesn't solve your problems, you need seriously to consider switching over to a Windows-based menu system or forgo running one of the memory-resident DOS applications.

Memory-resident anti-virus software can also trigger false alarms as it constantly monitors read/write activity. If this becomes too annoying, it may lead you to deactivate the program, which would result in reduced protection against viruses.

Expert Detection Systems

Expert detection systems are capable of detecting previously unknown viruses whose signatures might not be detectable by the scanning software or known viruses that the scanner is not programmed to recognize. These systems use a combination of techniques including checksum analysis. *Checksums* are the fingerprints of a file. *Checksum analysis* is a process that looks at the checksums of a file it suspects has a virus and compares them to the checksums that were recorded earlier when the system was clean. *Intelligent checksum analysis* is a more advanced process that can distinguish between changes to files that are normal and those that might be caused by a virus.

The best anti-virus applications include expert systems that can detect polymorphic viruses—viruses that mutate and take on false identities. Expert systems may run millions of tests trying to detect the presence of a virus. When the system finds one, it attempts to decrypt the virus and discover its true identity. At that point, it attempts to identify the virus by comparing its signature to the anti-virus software's inventory of known viruses.

WHICH ANTI-VIRUS SOFTWARE IS BEST?

Determining which anti-virus software is best is a difficult question to answer. You are immediately confronted with two problems:

1. The number of existing viruses in the wild grows continually. This makes it impossible for the different types of anti-virus software to remain 100 percent effective; and
2. There is no sure-fire method of testing the effectiveness of anti-virus software.

> ### What Are Viruses in the Wild?
>
> The phrase *viruses in the wild* refers to viruses that are out there in the real world as opposed to those that exist only in test laboratories. The phrase *virus zoo* is used to describe a library of viruses, not all of which exist in the wild.

The first challenge is met by choosing a company that provides periodic updates to their software. You should also check into virus alert sites on a regular basis. You will find that all the major anti-virus software developers offer update services; you can access virus alert sites online at the following locations:

- NCSA (National Computer Security Association) at *www.ncsa.com/alerts/*
- CERT advisories (Computer Emergency Response Teams) at Symantic Antivirus Research Center *www.symantec.com/avcenter/*

- Dr. Solomon's Virus Central at *www.drsolomon.com/vircen/*

TESTING AND CERTIFICATION OF SITES AND PRODUCTS

Some improvements have been made in testing anti-virus software. In the past, product testers determined the effectiveness of anti-virus software by testing it against zoo collections—viruses that existed in laboratories. These did not necessarily include the viruses that you and I would encounter in the real world. Now testers and reviewers are more concerned with the product's ability to defend against viruses occurring in the real world.

Joe Wells maintains a monthly electronic publication called the *WildList,* which is a cumulative list of viruses found in the wild. You can find copies of the *WildList* archived at site *ftp://ftp.ncsa.com/pub/virus/wildlist.* A complete archive of *WildLists* is available at the Virus Bulletin Web site *www.virusbtn.com/WildLists/index.html.* The *WildList* provides an expert accounting of the viruses being reported by 37 virus researchers worldwide. Virus Bulletin and NCSA are using the *WildList* to standardize the naming of viruses and to form the basis for their standard test-sets.

NCSA provides anti-virus certifications based on known viruses in the wild. NCSA also requires that products detect a minimum of 90 percent of the viruses they maintain in their own zoo. To learn more about NCSA certified products, go to their Web site at *www.ncsa.com/avpdcert.html.* Before purchasing anti-virus software, ask whether it is NCSA certified.

WHAT ARE THE LIMITATIONS OF ANTI-VIRUS SOFTWARE?

Even if you have a strong virus protection policy and you are running the best anti-virus software money can buy, you are not completely protected. Stealth viruses may avoid detection by some scanners. Stealth viruses do this by removing any clues that would tip-off the scanner when the file is opened for the scan operation. Some anti-virus software scanners support an anti-stealth defense that can detect what might be an unknown stealth virus at work.

A drawback of signature-based scanners is that they cannot stay current on virus detection. They offer no protection against viruses created after their inventory of signatures was last updated. Continuous updates help some, but there is still that window of opportunity for new viruses to infect your system between updates.

Remember, too, that polymorphic viruses can escape detection by altering the code string for which the scanner is searching.

WHAT IS MICROSOFT ANTI-VIRUS SOFTWARE?

If you are running Windows 3.1 and MS-DOS 6.x, you should find an anti-virus program called VSAFE in your DOS directory. (You should not use the VSAFE command when Windows is running.) VSAFE is a no-frills memory-resident program that monitors your PC for viruses and provides a warning when it finds one it recognizes. You can learn more about the capabilities of VSAFE by entering **help** at your DOS prompt and then looking under the topic **VSAFE**. The downside of relying on VSAFE is that it is incapable of detecting any of the newer viruses.

Resource Tip

VALERT-L is an electronic mailing list that posts warnings about viruses. To join, send an e-mail message to *listserv@lehigh.edu*. In the body of the message, type **sub valert-l <your name>**.

WHAT CAN YOU DO TO AVOID VIRUSES?

You cannot avoid viruses 100 percent of the time, but you can reduce your risks considerably by discovering what your vulnerabilities are and then closing them. Try to avoid these common pitfalls:

- **Forgetting to check floppy disks:** Most virus protection programs include a utility that runs in the background. If someone inadvertently inserts an infected floppy disk in a floppy disk drive, for example, the memory resident anti-virus program is likely to catch it and sound an alarm. If you elect to disarm this feature because it consumes too much memory, you must remember to scan floppy disks manually.

- **Downloading from the Internet:** If you download files from the Internet, first place the files in a temporary directory and scan them for viruses. When you purchase your anti-virus software, make sure that it is capable of scanning compressed files. Most of the files you download from the Internet will be zipped.

- **Allowing individuals to use their own floppy disks:** When library patrons, staff, teachers, students, or friends bring in their own floppy disks to use in private or shared PCs, scan the floppy disks for viruses before allowing them to be used.

- **Forgetting to back up important data:** If you have files that are difficult or impossible to replace, back them up so you can reload them if the original files get destroyed by a virus.

- **Not protecting your floppy disks:** Some viruses are memory-resident viruses and will infect your floppy disk when you access it on the infected system. You can prevent the virus from copying itself to your floppy disk by write-protecting it. You do this on 3.5–inch floppies by sliding the little switch in the corner so that the write-protect hole is open.

- **Leaving disks in floppy disk drives:** The only way to infect your PC with a boot sector virus is by attempting to boot from an infected floppy disk. Therefore, before you turn your computers on, always check to see whether someone has left a disk in one of the drives. If you find one, remove it.

- **Being caught without a boot disk:** You may need to reboot your PC with a clean system disk. Make sure that you have one available at all times. The details of creating emergency boot disks were covered in Chapter 2.

- **Using a macro to open your Word files:** Microsoft suggests opening files without macros to prevent macro viruses from spreading.

- **Not using the best anti-virus program for your system:** If you run Windows 95, you need a proper Windows 95 32–bit anti-virus package for full protection. If you are running DOS and Windows 3.x, you are better off using a product that supports Windows and DOS, not just DOS.

- **No protection at home:** Make sure that your staff's

home systems are protected as well as their PCs at work.

- **Your PCs boot from floppy disk drives:** Go into CMOS and change the PC setup so that your system first looks at the hard drive to boot up instead of the floppy disk drive. (If you need to boot up with a clean system disk, go back into CMOS and temporarily re-enable booting from the floppy disk drive.)

HOW CAN YOU TELL WHEN A VIRUS HAS INFECTED YOUR PC?

Because your anti-virus software is only as good as the last update, there is a chance that you might come under attack by an unknown virus. Here are some of the effects you may notice when an infected program file is launched:

- An unexpected screen message appears
- You lose data or lose access to your data on a server
- You have trouble printing a file
- Files become corrupted
- Your system crashes
- You have trouble saving files

WHAT SHOULD YOU DO WHEN YOU DETECT A VIRUS?

If you suspect a virus has infected your PC, follow these general procedures:

1. Stop whatever you are doing and close any open applications.
2. Shut the computer off and leave it off for a moment. Do not press the reset button or reboot the computer by pressing CTRL+ALT+DEL.
3. Get your emergency boot disk and make sure that it is write-protected. Insert it in the floppy disk drive (usually drive A) and then turn the computer back on. (Instructions on how to make a clean startup disk were presented at the end of Chapter 1.)
   a. If after booting with this disk you find a virus in memory, it is likely that the boot floppy disk is infected and you cannot use it for this operation.
   b. Do not try to disinfect your PC when there is a virus active in memory. It will interfere with the process and possibly infect more files.
4. Once the system is back on and running, scan the C drive for viruses according to the instructions that came along with your anti-virus software. To "scan" the C drive means running an anti-virus program that searches for the existence of viruses on the hard drive. (When you install most anti-virus software, it asks you whether you want to make an emergency startup disk. During this process, some programs create a disk that when run, automatically begin scanning for viruses after bootup.)
   a. You can run the scan operation from a floppy disk that is write-protected.
   b. If the virus is a stealth virus, extra precautions must be taken because they are very difficult to

detect. Once stealth viruses are memory resident, they can hide themselves on the hard drive and floppy disk. This is why it is important to be sure that the virus is not in memory when you scan a hard drive or floppy disk.

c. For additional tips on how to remove a particular virus, refer to the online virus databases presented in Table 6–1. The databases maintained by McAfee and the U.S. Department of Energy are two of the most comprehensive. The excerpt presented in Figure 6–1 is taken from Department of Energy's database.

Table 6–1: Virus encyclopedias on the Web	
McAfee Virus Information Library	www.mcafee.com/support/ techdocs/vinfo/f_1.html
Semantic Virus Information Database	www.symantec.com/avcenter/ vinfodb.html
CIAC Virus Database (U.S. Department of Energy's Computer Incident Advisory Capability)	ciac.llnl.gov/ciac/ CIACVirusDatabase.html
F-Prot computer virus information	www.datafellows.com/vir-info/
Cheyenne Virus Encyclopedia	www.cheyenne.com/security/ virdesc.html

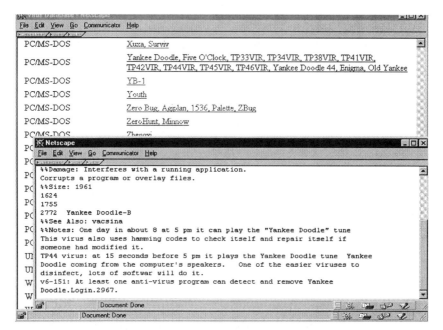

Figure 6–1: Information on the Yankee Doodle virus supplied by CIAC's virus database

5. After the virus has been removed, shut down your PC and then restart it. (When a virus is detected, your scanning software usually cleans, or "fixes" the infected file by removing the virus. Sometimes files are so damaged by a virus that they cannot be restored to their original state. This is why backing up critical information is so important. You may be required to delete a file in order to remove the virus from your system.)

6. Scan all floppy disks you may have been using to prevent re-infecting the hard disk with an infected program on a floppy disk.

7. Lastly, if the scanning software does not successfully remove a virus from an infected file, you must take the necessary steps to delete the infected file. (Refer to the instructions included with your anti-virus software for properly deleting infected files.) Remember which files you delete so you can replace them with uninfected copies.

WHAT ARE GOOD TIMES, DEEYENDA, AND IRINA?

Good Times, Deeyenda, and Irina are all virus hoaxes. They are sometimes referred to as junk-mail viruses because they are myths spread around the Net via e-mail. To learn more about these and other Internet virus hoaxes, check out Dr. Solomon's Virus Central Web site at *www.drsolomon.com/vircen/*. Click on the link labeled **Virus Central**. The Good Times virus has its own FAQ(list of frequently asked questions with answers) stored on the FTP server at *ftp://ftp.netcom.com/pub/ne/netcom/*.

OTHER COMPUTER MALWARE (MALICIOUS SOFTWARE)

Other programs besides viruses can be a threat to computer security and data integrity. These include Trojan Horses, worms, and logic bombs.

A *Trojan Horse* is a program that appears to be harmless, such as a game or utility, but when you run it, it can perform destructive acts in the background without your knowledge. It differs from a virus in that it does not reproduce.

A *worm* is a program that spreads itself around, but not by attaching itself to code such as viruses do. It travels over network connections and is normally not associated with PCs. Rather, it can drain the resources of host computers by consuming available memory.

A *logic bomb* modifies a computer program so that, under certain conditions, it executes in some different way. Normal testing does not reveal a logic bomb. Only when the special conditions occur does the program perform differently than normal. Logic bombs are sometimes used to embezzle funds. Code is added to a program so that it increases a person's payroll check by some small amount each month. Or, a logic bomb can be used to destroy a file or randomly alter data in one cell of a spreadsheet.

INTRODUCING VIRUSAFE 95

ViruSafe 95 is a virus protection application produced by EliaShim. A demonstration version of this software is included on the CD-ROM that accompanies this book. (To try out this program and other free anti-virus applications, go to the AV directory on the accompanying CD-ROM.) If you were to list the most important features in virus protection software, ViruSafe would include them all. One of the most notable is that it is NCSA-certified—a feature you should look for before you invest in any anti-virus software. This means it can detect 100 percent of the viruses found in the wild and at least 90 percent of the viruses maintained in NCSA's virus zoo.

Knowing that EliaShim has developed a good scanner is reassuring, but as I stated earlier, scanning for virus signatures alone does not offer optimal protection. ViruSafe, like other top-shelf anti-virus products, also scans for unknown viruses and watches for any illegal behavior that could signal a virus attack. ViruSafe accomplishes this by utilizing integrity checking (also called *checksum analysis*) and heuristic analysis. (These processes are described earlier in the chapter.)

The online scanner called *Protect* is always running in the background checking for viruses. You can set Protect to automatically scan files, floppy disks, and to notify you of any virus like activities that are taking place. The offline scanner enables you to check for viruses according to a pre-set configuration.

Resource Tip

The Computer Virus Research Center located in Indianapolis, Indiana, maintains a computer virus help desk at *iw1.indyweb.net/~cvhd/*.

ViruSafe's Encyclopedia of Virus Information

One area in which ViruSafe does not yet measure up to its competitors is in the depth of information it provides on individual viruses. Anti-virus software usually includes a searchable database of all the viruses known in the wild as part of the application. Entries typically include a description of the virus, symptoms to look for, and how to remove it. For example, where ViruSafe offers this generic description of symptoms for a virus called ADA:

> "Malfunction of the computer, slowdown of the computer activity, clogging up free space on the disk, destruction of hard disk data, etc."

McAfee offers this:

> "The following text strings are found in infected files:
> COMMAND.COM
> PCCILLIN.COM
> PCCILLIN.IMG
> HATI-HATI!!ADA VIRUS DISINI!!Delete
>
> Systems infected with Ada experience a slow clicking sound, emitted from the system speaker. This clicking occasionally changes in pitch. The user may also receive a "Disk full" error even though the disk the user is attempting to write to is not actually full."

And the McAfee description continues with how ADA infects files and how to remove ADA.

Installing ViruSafe 95

I installed ViruSafe 95 on a Windows 95 machine and a Windows 3.x/DOS version of ViruSafe on a PC running Windows 3.1. Installation went smoothly and the accompanying manual was helpful in getting things configured properly.

If you are installing VirusSafe on an older PC with the 5.25–inch drive designated as the boot drive, you may run into a problem because the program assumes the boot drive will be a 3.5–inch drive. You can fix this by swapping the drive cables inside the system unit and by changing the CMOS settings, but be certain to have the okay of your system administrator before proceeding.

WHERE CAN YOU FIND INFORMATION ABOUT VIRUSES ON THE NET?

You will no doubt be overwhelmed by the amount of information on the Net pertaining to viruses. On the darker side, there are Web sites maintained by hackers that offer virus libraries and virus production software. Kids that access these sites run a high risk of downloading virus-infected software to public access PCs. (A procedure is described in Chapter 8 that prevents patrons from downloading files from the Web using Netscape Navigator.)

Table 6–2 lists some of the better-known virus information repositories on the Net. These sites provide information on virus-types, how to remove viruses, anti-virus software, virus alerts, and more. For current reviews of anti-virus software, be sure to check out *PC Magazine Online*.

Table 6–2: Virus information centers on the Internet

Name	Address
Central Command Incorporated	www.command-hq.com/
Check-It	www.checkit.com/tshome.htm
Cheyenne Security Center	www.cheyenne.com/
DataFellows Virus Information Center	www.datafellows.com/vir-info/
David Harley's Anti-Virus Home Page	www.webworlds.co.uk/dharley/
Dr. Solomon's Virus Central	www.drsolomon.com/vircen/
EliaShim	www.eliashim.com/
IBM Anti-Virus Online	www.av.ibm.com/current/ FrontPage/
McAfee Virus Pages	www.mcafee.com/
National Computer Security Association	www.ncsa.com
NIST Virus Information Page	csrc.nist.gov/virus/
Norman Data Defense Systems	www.norman.com
PC Magazine Online - Reviews of Anti-Virus Utilities	www8.zdnet.com/pcmag features/utility/av/_open.htm
Sophos Virus Information Page	www.sophos.com/virusinfo/
Stiller Research Virus Information	www.stiller.com/
Symantec Antivirus Research Center	www.symantec.com/avcenter/ index.html
Thunderbyte	www.thunderbyte.com
Touchstone - Makers of PC-cillin	www.checkit.com/tshome.htm

Chapter 7

Methods and Procedures for Maintaining Privacy

*Privacy is absolutely essential to
maintaining a free society.*
—Benno C. Schmidt, Jr., interview,
The Christian Science Monitor,
December 5, 1986

In Chapter 7, I explore computer security as it pertains to privacy—keeping computer data secure and shielded from prying eyes. I explain how to password-protect Word documents and files in general. I also examine file shredders—special applications that wipe your disks clean of sensitive files.

One of the most inexpensive and effective methods of protecting the privacy of your stored data and e-mail is encryption. In this chapter, I explain how encryption software protects your privacy and protects your data against tampering and forgery. Some encryption systems can even guarantee the authenticity of the information that is being sent and received, using a tool called a *digital signature*.

WHAT IS ENCRYPTION?

Encryption is a process that takes plain text and scrambles it so that it becomes unreadable, as shown in Figure 7–1. This scrambled text is referred to as *ciphertext*. Before you can read ciphertext, you have to decipher it with a secret *key*. When you apply the key to plain text, the text is encrypted and when you apply the key to ciphertext text, the text is deciphered. A key's length is described in terms of bits. The longer a key is, the more difficult it is to crack.

HOW DO YOU ENCRYPT DATA?

There are two systems used for encrypting data: Single key and two key encryption.

Single Key Systems

In a *single key system* (also called *secret key* or *symmetric encryption*), the encryption key and the decryption key are the same. The problem with using single key encryption for e-mail transmissions is that you have to communicate the decryption key to the person receiving your message.

When you transmit a message explaining the key, there is a chance that the key could be intercepted by a third party. A safe way to let someone know what a key is, is to do it in person. If you are encrypting data on your own hard drive, exchanging secret keys with other individuals will not be a concern.

```
                          Plaintext
When, in the course of human events, it becomes necessary for one people to dissolve the political bonds
which have connected them with another, and to assume among the powers of the earth, the separate and
equal station to which the laws of nature and of nature's God entitle them, a decent respect to the opinions
of mankind requires that they should declare the causes which impel them to the separation.
                         Ciphertext
š,□□;("ùKOè&ßÇÞÕŒwïP¼M;ïŒ»□¤ Šó+Óa¥9t±9fO□P¹Hã Gz3{¶"□¾ÍMö%œhcù§5□0F-
áà□Kü□*ï½-:„©µ¾ô&‡í£□ÓqÅ]'>□"J|øÿÞv:†Lÿ-¿U±y—6ÊÔÝs□.Ýí□`Ñþ□ ÞÒ$ÝÂ°à]),□□□ó$...-
Š¡óz□ÂnÝç4Ë©ŒŸƒ,Ò2°ÂkEM|□[<õ!B7q"'B'að—PY□FŸÌ"e½□É¡ë5Ôâ}"h□ßQûµ6à"¶÷Û□□ízX'è—
œb□ŠÖ>£5g®nI"•□»m~xpvaáÉòy·Ú‡¶6MâÑ□‡UÇn*S<D°ây¤]¼$Ó¼%oþG㽄"\□ð-□Jq□tO&ÈÂ)†½
□œùþ†d-;$ý~xNwhdg³hWŠ^uOimã*>□H\Õê²{□Óà¶è□□ƒÁ úÛw□ÐÛØ²□;E>PÐDí"´¼&Q□□d]Û7{y□:
|□nÀK"úÒP:y~tŠ3ÒÝù□:¤"□ø¼□j'□□p-½àsè-™>]]N©¡4q
```

Figure 7–1: Text scrambled with encryption software

Computer Underground Digest

Cu Digest (Computer Underground Digest) at *sun.soci.niu.edu/*
%7Ecudigest/ is a weekly e-journal of debates, news, research, and discussions on legal, social, and other issues
related to computer culture. Topics include encryption,
hacking, and security.

Two Key Systems

Two key systems (also called *asymmetric key systems*) use
a public key for encrypting data and a private key for decrypting data. For example, if you have a friend that wants
to send you something confidential over the Internet, you
tell that person what your public key is and he or she uses
it to create an encrypted e-mail message. When you receive
the message, you decrypt it with your private key—the key
that only you know.

Similarly, if you want to send a private communication
to your friend, you encrypt it with your private key and
he or she decrypts it with the public key you supplied. The
other person does not need to know your private key. PGP
(Pretty Good Privacy) is an example of a two key system.

Cyberlaw Encyclopedia

The Cyberlaw Encyclopedia at *www.gahtan.com/techlaw/ crypto.htm* is a metasite for information relating to cryptography. This site offers access to full-text articles, legislative information, cases, and other Web resources, such as the *Cryptography Export Control Archives*.

WHY SHOULD YOU ENCRYPT DATA?

There are two reasons you might find it advantageous to encrypt data:

1. To prevent unauthorized access to information stored locally
2. To prevent the interception of information transmitted via e-mail

PREVENTING UNAUTHORIZED ACCESS

If you share a computer with another person, you may have files that you do not want others reading; for example, employee information. Corporate libraries may have information a competitor would like to see, such as research results or plans for a new product. If these files were encrypted, they would not be accessible by a casual observer.

PREVENTING INTERCEPTION

Protecting sensitive information when it is being transmitted over a network is another concern. Theoretically, anyone on your network can intercept and read data passing between your computer and another computer. Encryption offers a secure means of corresponding with others via e-mail about issues you would like to keep private. If you transmit an encrypted message over a network and it is intercepted before it reaches its destination, the inceptor will not be able to make any sense of it. Encryption assures you that no one reads your e-mail unless they hold the necessary key.

FAQ on Cryptography

Frequently Asked Questions About Today's Cryptography can be viewed on RSA Laboratories' Web site at *www.rsa.com/rsalabs/newfaq/foreword.htm*. RSA is an encryption technology that is used in a number of applications including Netscape Navigator, Lotus Notes, Microsoft Windows, and many other products.

ARE SOME CRYPTOSYSTEMS BETTER THAN OTHERS?

The system used for encrypting and decrypting data is called a *cryptosystem* or *encryption algorithm*. The security of a cryptosystem usually depends on the secrecy of the keys rather than the secrecy of the underlying instructions or "algorithms" that create the cryptosystem itself. These are usually completely public.

Should Teachers and Librarians Be Concerned?

Teachers and librarians generally are not concerned with the highest level of security that could keep governments and large corporations out of their private files. In most situations, the simpler cryptosystems with codes that can be broken by amateur cryptographers will do. Kremlin, a shareware cryptosystem for Windows 95 created by Mark Rosen, offers eight algorithms to choose from. They range from simple (ASCII and Vigenere) to moderately advanced (DES, NewDES, and Safer) to very advanced (Blowfish, IDEA, and pseudo-RC4). You can download a copy of Kremlin by visiting Kremlin's Web page at *www.geocities.com/SiliconValley/Pines/2690/kremlin.html.*

If by the time you read this, Kremlin's site has moved, try using Archie and search on the file name *krem106.zip* (the current version of Kremlin 1.06).

What Exactly Are These Encryption Algorithms?

Encryption algorithms simply are methods of scrambling data. There are only a few encryption algorithms around and they have names like IDEA, RSA, DES, Triple DES, RC2, and RC5. When you review the various encryption programs that are available, for example, PGP (Pretty Good Privacy), product descriptions usually include a description of the underlying technology that is being used. For example, you might read something like, "PGP uses RSA technology for authentication." It helps to know that RSA encryption (named after the three gentlemen who discovered RSA: Rivest, Shamir, and Adleman) is unique in that it operates using a pair of keys—one private and one public. Programs that are built on IDEA (International

Data Encryption Algorithm) or DES (Data Encryption Standard) technology use single key cryptography.

WHAT IS AUTHENTICATION?

Authentication is the process of verifying someone's identity. For example, I have two keys, a public key and a private key. In this scenario, suppose that you also have a public and private key. If I want to verify that you are who you say you are, I do it by sending you an encrypted e-mail message. I first encrypt my message with my own secret key, thus creating a digital signature, and then I encrypt it a second time with your public key. Then I send you the message.

When you receive the message, you apply these same steps, but in reverse order. You decrypt the message first using your own secret key and then using my public key. Only you could have read this message and only I could have sent it.

WHAT IS A DIGITAL SIGNATURE?

The term *digital signature* is used in a couple of different ways. Usually it means that the holder of a public key has the ability to verify where information comes from and who sent it. As in the example given above, you decrypted the e-mail message with your own private key to validate the "signature" and then applied my public key to verify that I sent the message.

On the Web, you are given a warning dialog box when you access an insecure site. You get these warnings because the site does not have a digital signature for the ActiveX control or JavaScript on its page. When you access a site for the first time with a digital signature, the signature is presented to you in the form of a certificate.

You can get your own digital signature from companies like VeriSign at *digitalid.versign.com*. (More on certificates in Chapter 8 under the heading "How Do You Know If You Are Connecting to a Secure Site?")

A company called PenOp applies a more literal interpretation of the term *signature*. PenOp uses specially-designed software to capture the signing event and then attaches the signature to a document. It is the digital equivalent of a handwritten signature.

To learn more about PenOp's basic components and pricing, visit their Web site at *www.penop.com*. To see a demonstration of how PenOp works, check out the PenOp Acrobat plug-in movie that is included with the software accompanying this book. (Look in the folder labeled *Digital Signatures* for a file named ADDEMO.EXE.)

WHAT IS PGP?

PGP (Pretty Good Privacy) is an encryption program originally created by Philip Zimmermann. It uses public key cryptography to protect the privacy of your files and is the *de facto* standard for Internet e-mail encryption. There are freeware and commercial versions of PGP available in the U.S. and Canada.

WHERE CAN I GET PGP?

The Massachusetts Institute of Technology (MIT) distributes the freeware versions of PGP at *web.mit.edu/network/pgp.html*. Your choices include:

- PGP Freeware 5.0 Installer for Windows 95 and NT
- MSDOS Executable Release, PGP 2.6.2

Tip for DOS Users

The file you download is named *pgp262.zip*. Place it in its own directory and then use PKUNZIP to uncompress the *pgp262.zip* file, using the command

    pkunzip –d pgp262

Inside, you will find another zip file named *pgp262i.zip*, which contains most of the files. Unzip *pgp262i.zip* with the command **pkunzip -d pgp262i**

Instructions on how to use PGP for DOS can be found in the DOC subdirectory on the CD-ROM. Look for *pgpdoc1.txt* and *pgpdoc2.txt*.

If you install the DOS version available from MIT, you can also install a graphical user interface shell to make PGP a little easier to use. There are a few of these shells available. You can pick one of the following:

- WPGP (shareware) available from *www.panix.com/~jgostl/wpgp/*
- Private Idaho (freeware) available from *www.eskimo.com/~joelm/pi.html*

Freeware versions are available to U.S. citizens in the U.S. and Canadian citizens in Canada. The freeware versions of PGP do not include technical support from PGP, Inc.

You can learn more about the commercial version of PGP at PGP, Inc.'s Web site at *www.pgp.com/*. For information on the international versions of PGP, check out the International PGP home page at *www.ifi.uio.no/pgp/*.

Exporting Encryption Software

The U.S. government's policies regarding the export of encryption software forbids the export of encryption technology without government approval. Ordinarily, approval is not granted unless the key length is 48 bits or less. The government has been under steady attack for this restriction because books explaining cryptographic algorithms are published and exchanged freely and the techniques used for creating algorithms are well known outside the U.S.

HOW DO YOU INSTALL PGP ON A WINDOWS 95 MACHINE?

Installing PGP for Windows 95 is intuitive, but I will go over a few points that are not covered in the online documentation. I will not be discussing how to use PGP to encrypt your documents; that is covered pretty well in Philip R. Zimmermann's *The Official PGP User's Guide* (ISBN: 0-262-74017-6) and William Stallings' *Protect Your Privacy: A Guide for PGP Users* (ISBN: 0-13-185596-4).

Downloading PGP

Go to the MIT PGP Freeware distribution site on the Web to get a copy of PGP Freeware 5.0 Installer for Windows 95. Download the file, which is called *pgpinstall.exe*, to a temporary directory. When it is finished downloading, open Windows Explorer, go to the directory in which *pgpinstall.exe* is stored and double-click on the file name. This unpacks the files that are used for setup.

Going through the Setup Process

When you come to the registration screen, you are prompted for a serial number. You can ignore this by clicking the **Next** button. By default, PGP will install itself in the C:\Program Files\PGP\PGP50 subdirectory. You then are given the option of choosing which components to install; for example, plug-ins for Eudora and Microsoft Exchange. Click the boxes for the components in which you are interested.

Do You Already Have Keyring Files?

The setup program will ask you if you have existing public and private keyrings. If you do not, click on the button labeled **No** and you will be prompted to run a program called PGPkeys. This program walks you through the steps of generating a key pair, which consists of a public key and a private key.

Creating Your Public and Private Keys

The first step in creating your public and private keys is entering your full name and e-mail address. Next, you are asked whether you want to generate a DSS/Diffie-Hellman or RSA key. You do not have a real choice here. The former has already been picked for you by default.

The next decision you have to make is how large you want to make your keys. Bigger keys are more secure, but take longer to process. For most school and library applications, 1024 bits should suffice.

Next, you must create a password to protect your private key. If you make the password less than eight characters long, the program tells you so and asks whether you really want to compromise the security of your key by using such a password. PGP then generates your key pair.

Sending Your Key to a Keyserver

If you are online, you can take this opportunity to send your new key to a *public keyserver*, the central site that makes your public key available to anyone who is interested. To get started, you can go to the pull-down Help menu and read all about encrypting and decrypting data. When you are finished and you close down PGPkeys, you are asked whether you want to make a backup copy of your keyring files—something I would recommend doing because hard drives do crash from time to time.

Powerful applications and user friendliness usually do not go hand in hand, and PGP is no exception. Be ready to spend the good part of a day, if not longer, learning how to use this program. If all you want to do is encrypt files stored on your personal computer, be sure to go with a simpler, single key system. You usually can have single key systems like Cryptext installed and running in a matter of minutes.

HOW TO INSTALL AND RUN CRYPTEXT

Cryptext is a Windows 95 file encryption program developed by Nick Payne. You can find a copy of Cryptext on the CD-ROM that accompanies this book. Look for a file named *CRYPTEXT.ZIP* located in the CRYPTO directory. After you unzip the file, right-click on the file named *CRYPTEXT.INF* and select **Install** from the popup menu. Installing Cryptext adds **Encrypt** and **Decrypt** items to the menu that appears when you right-click on files and directories in Windows Explorer.

Cryptext runs in two different modes. One mode uses an agent and the other mode encrypts and decrypts without an agent. Using an agent is more sophisticated and takes a little more setup time, but provides a higher level of security. You can learn more about these modes by running the *cryptic.exe* file and reading the Cryptext Help files. Basically, an *agent* is a file that defines a set of rotors (*rotors* are sequences of 8–bit bytes created at random and stored as files, also known as *keys*).

The easiest way to run Cryptext is to open Explorer and select a file to encrypt. When the file's name is highlighted, right-click the mouse and select **Encrypt**. Lastly, enter a password. When you want to decrypt the file, right-click on the file name and select **Decrypt** from the menu. When you enter the proper password, Cryptext decodes the file.

SECURE FILE SHREDDING

Data recovery techniques are sophisticated enough to re-cover deleted files; that is, files that you remove with the standard DOS **del** or **erase** commands. File recovery is a simple process because **del** really removes only the file's name from your disk's index. The contents of your file re-main on the disk. If you want to delete sensitive data and be sure that it is deleted for good, you should use a spe-cial file deletion utility called a *file shredder*. File shred-ders are specialized utilities designed to delete your files securely by overwriting data with zeros and ones and then with random garbage. *File wiping* is another term used to describe this process.

Various programs are available for shredding files. One program called MICRO-ZAP from New Technologies, Inc., is available on the CD-ROM that accompanies this book. MICRO-ZAP was designed for law enforcement and military use to erase sensitive data stored in computer files. MICRO-ZAP runs under DOS. Three other file shredders also are included on the CD-ROM: Wipe v3.20 developed by Enver J. Berkes, WIPE v1.1 developed by Vesa Kolhinen, and Dustin Cook's NUKE. Kolhinen's program uses certain U.S. government rules for shredding files. When you use the /G switch in your command, for ex-ample, you run the official "government wipe". This stan-dard states that you should overwrite the data with ones and zeros three times and then overwrite the data with ran-dom junk.

PASSWORD PROTECTING SCREEN SAVERS

Screen savers are used to prevent images from burning into your screen. They also prevent others from reading what is on your screen while you are away from your computer. Windows 3.x and Windows 95 both offer screen saver password features. When someone presses a key or moves the mouse while your screen saver is activated, a window pops up asking for a password. You access the screen saver settings in Windows 3.x through the Desktop module in the Control Panel. In Windows 95, you can set up your screen saver and password by clicking on the Display icon in Control Panel.

Setting Timers on Screen Savers

Screen savers normally are activated by setting a timer. After three minutes, for example, the screen saver activates if you haven't touched your keyboard or mouse for that period of time. If you get up and walk away from your computer, there would be a three-minute window of opportunity open during which time someone could come along and access your system before the screen saver activated.

Double-clicking to Activate Your Screen Saver

There are programs that provide a solution for this situation. SCRSaver is a Freeware Windows 95 program developed by Jin Gang that is included on the CD-ROM accompanying this book. Look in the MISC directory for the file named *SCRSAVER.ZIP*. When you run *Scrsaver.exe*, the program appears as an icon in the system tray. If you have to leave your computer unattended, you can double-click on the icon, which immediately activates your screen saver. If you have not configured a screen saver, double-clicking on the icon opens the Control Panel and gives you an opportunity to do so. Be sure to set your password at this time for added security. To find a copy, search on the file named *scrsaver.zip* at *www.shareware.com*.

You can download another program with similar features, called SAVERCTL, from *www.shareware.com*. To find SAVERCTL at this site, use their search engine to search on the file named *saverctl.zip*. As with SCRSaver, SAVERCTL starts your screen saver immediately when you double-click on the program icon in the system tray. SAVERCTL also monitors *hot corners*—areas on the screen that you click to activate and disable the program when the system tray is hidden.

Hacking Password-Protected Screen Savers

Hackers will try a couple of things to get around your screen saver password. If they can sneak in before your screen saver activates, they open *control.ini* with a text editor and delete the ScreenSaver entry. If your screen saver is activated, they reboot your system and then edit the *control.ini* file before your screen saver activates. Your best defense against this is to implement a bootup password. *PC Security*, a program described later in this chapter, enables you to have a secure screen saver load as part of the bootup process. This prevents hackers from removing the ScreenSaver entry in *control.ini* by simply rebooting the PC.

PASSWORD PROTECTION AND ACCESS RESTRICTIONS

Secure menu systems, like those introduced in Chapter 5, attempt to enforce security by controlling access to programs through menu choices. Password protection software uses a different approach. These applications enable you to place "locks" on individual files. Under these systems, you can access a locked file only if you know the correct password. Some packages offer other features as well. WinSafe, for example, provides a user-friendly front-end to the Windows 95 policy editor. Depending on which level of security you are seeking, these applications can be used as stand-alone security measures or used in conjunction with secure menu systems.

Securing Word for Windows Documents

In this section, I show you how to use passwords to stop others from opening and changing your MS Word documents. The correct password must be provided before a password-protected file can be opened. Here you learn how to set passwords on Word for Windows files and crack the passwords if you forget them.

PASSWORD-PROTECTING A DOCUMENT

1. Open the document you want to protect.
2. Click on **File** menu and choose **Save As**.
3. If you have not already named the file, name it now by typing a name in the **File Name** box.
4. Next, click on the **Options** button.

5. In the **Protection Password** box, type a password and then click on **OK**. Your password can consist of up to 15 characters. The password will appear as asterisks (*) when you type it. Passwords are case-sensitive, so remember where you use upper- and lowercase letters.
6. After you click on **OK**, Word prompts you to confirm the password. Type it in again and then click on **OK**.
7. Click on the **OK** button to save the document.

The next time you open your password-protected document, you will have to type in the password before you are permitted to view the file.

PROTECTING A DOCUMENT

If you want to make it possible for others to access and view a document, but keep them from adding or deleting text, you can protect it by using the Protect Document command found in the Tools menu. Click on **Tools,** choose **Protect Document,** and then click on **Protect document for annotations.** Now other users can open the document, but they can make comments only by using annotations. To annotate the document, the user must click on **Insert** and then choose **Annotation.**

CRACKING PASSWORD-PROTECTED FILES

If you set a password on a Word for Windows document and then forget it, all is not lost. Fauzan Mirza wrote a program called WFWCD (Word for Windows Cracker

Demo) that tries to figure out the password. WFWCD works best if the password-protected document contains more than 300 bytes of data (300 characters, or roughly 60 words), and consists primarily of lowercase letters. Here is how WFWCD works.

Take a text file you have created in Word for Windows and password-protect it. Now run WFWCD and see whether you can crack the password. Follow these steps:

1. Copy the file named *wpasscrk.zip* from the PSSWRD directory found on the CD-ROM that accompanies this book.
2. When you unzip WFWCD, you find two files: *WFWCD.TXT* and *WFWCD.EXE*. The file named *WFWCD.EXE* runs the program. Go to the directory on your hard drive where you stored a copy of *WFWCD.EXE*. Type **wfwcd** and press **ENTER**.
3. The cracker program prompts you to enter the document path. Let's say the encrypted document, called *kidchat.doc*, resides in the subdirectory C:\APPS\KIDS. At the **Enter document path:** prompt, enter **c:\apps\kids\kidchat.doc**

The results will look something like the output shown in Figure 7–2. This figure shows the first few lines of decrypted text and the forgotten password (**10#bag**) which is displayed at the bottom of the screen.

PC Security

PC Security, developed by Tropical Software, offers several levels of protection ranging from locking files and re-

```
┌──────────────────────────────────────────────────────────────────┐
│  Auto    ▾  □  ▨  ▣  ▥  ▨  ▤  A                                    │
├──────────────────────────────────────────────────────────────────┤
Word for Windows Password Cracker (R8)
Copyright by Fauzan Mirza, August 1996

KIDCHAT.DOC: Word 6 for Windows document

Kids Chatting

Its hard to escape the fact that kids of all ages like chatting online.  Chattin
g is real-time conversations taking place on the Internet.  Kids talk to each ot
her by typing messages at their keyboards and listen by reading what thers type.
    Its kind of like talking on the phone, except much less expensive.  Two indivi
duals can talk, or many conversations can  take place between many people all at
the same time.  If you have an Internet computer in the childrens services area
of your library, chat is one of the services kids will ask for and one you can s
upport.

To use chat--also referred to as IRC which stands for Internet Relay Chat--you m
ust connect to a chat server.  Chat servers are applications that manage all of
the conversations going on simultaneously in a place called a chat room or chann
el.  Everyone in a particular chat room sees what ever

DOCUMENT PASSWORD: 10doag

C:\TEMP>
```

Figure 7–2: Word for Windows Cracker "cracks" a Word for Windows password

stricting access to Control Panel to removing the Run command from the Windows 95 Start menu and disabling the DOS prompt.

You can find a copy of PC Security on the CD-ROM that accompanies this book. Look in the directory named ACCESS for a file called *pcsec16.zip* (16–bit version) or *pcsec32.zip* (32–bit version). Installing PC Security takes less than a minute and it includes an uninstall feature that makes it easy to remove in case you decide not to use it.

PC Security offers five different modes of operation. You access each mode by clicking on its corresponding button on the toolbar.

   1. **File Lock Screen**—This screen allows you to browse through all of the directories and files on your hard drive and view which files are locked and which are

unlocked. This screen also enables you to select files from your hard drive and add them to a locked or unlocked file list.

2. **Window Lock Screen**—This screen lists all of the various windows available on your PC and allows you to disable them or disable them and make them invisible.

3. **Shortcut/Program Lock Screen**—This screen makes it possible to browse the Desktop, Start button, and your hard drive, locking and unlocking any program you wish.

4. **Explorer Control Screen**—This screen is used to limit various access points to the system, Start menu, display properties, and DOS operating environment. Examples of Start menu controls include **Remove Run and Find Commands**; Computer-related controls include **Hide Drives in My Computer** and **Don't Save Settings at Exit**; DOS-related controls include **Disable DOS Prompt** and **Disable DOS Applications**; controls related to the Display Properties control include **Hide Background Page** and **Hide Screen Saver** page; and the **For All Users** controls enable you to restrict access to such things as Control Panel, Printers, and Recycle Bin.

5. **Restrict System**—This screen allows you to set up a "Permitted Programs" list for public-access PCs. When activated, only the programs in the Permitted Programs list are allowed to run. Different users can be given different lists of permitted programs. Restricting the Default User is an important action to take. The Default User is the one that loads when you press the Cancel button at the Windows 95 bootup screen.

You can learn more about PC Security by visiting Tropical Software's Web site at *www.tropsoft.com* or by writing to them at 700 NW Gilman Blvd., Suite 345, Issaquah, WA 98027.

You can purchase copies of PC Security for Windows 3.1 and 95 for $34.95 by calling (425) 836–9270 or by sending e-mail to their sales department at *sales@tropsoft. com.*

GateWAY Password Protection

GateWAY 2.01, from Adafinn Software, Inc., is a basic security package that locks users out at bootup. In order for GateWAY's security features to be fully effective, you should go into your CMOS settings and change the boot sequence from A:-C: to C:-A:. This prevents hackers from breaking into your system by booting from a floppy disk. Also make sure that you have password protection on your CMOS setup. GateWAY's features include disabling F8 and F5 at bootup, disabling CTRL+BREAK during *autoexec.bat* bootup, and keyboard locking. You can find a copy of GateWAY on the CD-ROM that accompanies this book. Look in the MISC directory for a file named *Gatwy201.zip.*

Safetynet's StopLight PC

Safetynet, Inc., offers a product called StopLight that runs on Windows 95, Windows 3.x, and DOS workstations. StopLight 95 ELS is their entry-level security product for PCs and laptops that offers basic features, such as restricting unauthorized system changes and access to programs, and requiring individuals to login at bootup. StopLight 95 ELS supports up to 255 users per PC and each user can have his or her own unique security profile.

Their mid-range security product, called StopLight 95 PC, probably offers more features than most organizations need, such as full-disk encryption and the ability to set up audit logs. Auditing helps you log all logins, failures to log in, and other suspicious-looking activities that relate to access control. Maintaining and interpreting data for medium to small organizations is time-consuming and probably not worth the effort.

You can learn more about StopLight and download evaluation copies of their software by visiting Safetynet's Web site at *www.safe.net*. While you are there, you also might want to check out their DOS-based menu system named Drive-In Menu and their anti-virus software VirusNet. You can order StopLight 95 ELS online for $49.99 or order by phone by calling their customer service department at (800) 672–SAFE or (973) 467–1024.

Fortres 101 and Historian

Fortres Grand Corporation is the developer of Fortres 101, a desktop and file security system for Windows 3.x and Windows 95. Some of Fortres 101's features include preventing breakouts during bootup; exiting Windows; accessing the DOS prompt; changing printer and screen saver configurations; adding, deleting, or moving icons; and erasing or saving files on the hard disk.

Fortres Grand Corporation offers another product that may be of interest to teachers and librarians called Historian. Historian is a utility that tracks computer usage. If you are interested in tracking how much time patrons spend on certain applications, this program will record that information.

To learn more about Fortres 101 and Historian, visit their Web site at *www.fortres.com* or write to them at P.O. Box 888, Plymouth, IN 46653. For general information, send e-mail to *jpitsch@fortres.com*. You can order Fortres products online or by calling (800) 331–0372, (219) 935–3891, or FAX (800) 882–4381, (291) 935–3869. Fortres 101 educational pricing is $295.00 for every computer in a single building; corporate pricing is $395.00 for up to 50 computers in a single building.

Are Your Passwords Safe?

Are your passwords safe? One way to check the effectiveness of the passwords being used on your system is to run a program that tries to guess everyone's password. If the cracker program successfully guesses a password, you can temporarily disable the account to prevent an attacker from doing what you just did. When the user logs in, he or she will not be able to access the account until a new password is assigned.

Brute 2.0 is a UNIX password cracker designed to be run from DOS. You can find a copy at *www.accesspro.net/tekru/brute20.zip*. Star Cracker is another Unix password cracker that runs under DOS, Windows 95, and Unix. You can download a copy of StarCracker 1.01b from *www.chez.com/thes/starcrak.html*.

WinSafe

Would you like to forgo installing and managing a secure menu system and simply use the Windows 95 desktop as a front-end to applications? WinSafe, from Software Shelf International, Inc., makes this possible. It does the same thing the Windows 95 System Policy Editor is capable of doing (see Chapter 5 for details) except in a friendlier, easier to understand manner.

Like the System Policy Editor, WinSafe allows you to establish access restrictions to selected parts of Windows 95. Unlike the Policy Editor, WinSafe makes the job easier by providing you with such things as context-sensitive help, tooltips, and tabbed pages.

WinSafe has some practical applications in schools and libraries. In a networked environment, you can use WinSafe to force users to go through a validation process and to prevent file sharing by users. Another practical use would be on staff PCs. Although the public-access PCs could be running secure menu systems, staff would have access to more tools and resources working from the Windows 95 desktop. The system administrator's job would be made easier, however, if he or she were given centralized control over the security on each staff member's PC.

WinSafe offers more than 170 features for controlling user profiles, registries, and system policies including the ability to do the following:

- Customize start menus and desktops
- Hide drives in My Computer
- Hide items on the Desktop
- Disable the Shutdown command
- Disable save settings at exit

- Disable Registry editing tools
- Only run allowed Windows applications
- Disable the MS-DOS prompt

A single copy of WinSafe runs around $99.00, plus shipping and handling. You can learn more about WinSafe by writing to Software Shelf International, Inc., 931 McCue Ave., Bldg. #2, San Carlos, CA 94070, or by exploring their Web site at *www.softwareshelf.com*. WinSafe makes available a self-extracting demo version of their software that you can download from this site. You also have access to WinSafe's help manual—a 58Kb file in Word format. You can purchase their software online or you can call in your order at (800) 962–2290, (415) 631–8900, or FAX (415) 631–1430.

Chapter 8

Internet-Related Security Issues

Our watchword is security.
—William Pitt, Earl of Chatham, 1708–78

The Internet presents a whole new set of security problems for schools and libraries. When you connect your organization to the Internet, Internet hackers can begin probing your site looking for weaknesses. When a hacker discovers a way in—for example, an unprotected guest account or easily guessed password—news of the find travels fast to other hackers all around the world. Another security weakness that is inherent in the Internet is that data can be intercepted as it travels from one computer to another before reaching its destination.

Although hackers coming in from the outside are a concern, exploring this and the issues surrounding firewalls and secure servers is beyond the scope of this book. In Chapter 8, I focus on security issues surrounding Internet-related software running on PCs.

I begin by explaining what cookies are, identifying the

security risks associated with cookies, and discussing how you can prevent unauthorized information from being passed to your PC through cookies. I also explore which protocols are important for secure online transactions and what dangers, if any, are associated with Java and JavaScript. This is followed with a discussion on how to maintain your anonymity on the Net using The Anonymizer and anonymous remailers. I conclude by showing you how to tighten up security on Netscape Navigator by using a resource editor to "gray out" menu items.

WHAT IS A COOKIE?

A *cookie* is a file that is passed between a Web server and your Web browser. You send a packet of information to a server and the server sends you a cookie. The purpose of a cookie is to collect information or to identify who you are.

Some cookies remain in memory while others expire. Shopping sites, for example, sometimes use cookies to create a permanent record that contains your name and mailing address. The next time you visit that site, this information is passed back to the server. Cookies are also used to collect information that is later used for designing the content of a Web site.

WHERE ARE COOKIES STORED?

Cookies are stored in a file that resides on your personal computer. On Windows-based computers running Netscape 3.0, the file is called *cookies.txt* and it is stored in the Netscape folder. Earlier versions of Netscape name the file *.netscape-cookies* or *.netscape/cookies*. To view the contents of the cookies file, simply open it with a text editor like NotePad. The top of your text document should look something like this:

> Netscape HTTP Cookie Filehttp://www.netscape.com/ newsref/std/cookie_spec.htmlThis is a generated file! Do not edit.

When you first look at your *cookies.txt* file, you are likely to find several lines of garbled text following the line, "This is a generated file! Do not edit." This is the coded data that certain Web sites are storing on your computer.

DO COOKIES POSE A SECURITY RISK?

Theoretically, you could acquire a cookie that logs every site you visit and logs information that passes between your PC and the server, such as your address and credit card information. You would not necessarily know who is on the other end of the connection doing it or what they were using the information for. There are, at present, strict limitations built into cookie programming standards. For example, only the server that passes the cookie to your PC can read and use the cookie; no more than 300 cookies can be stored on your PC at any one time and no more than 20 from a single site; and cookies can be no bigger than 4 kilobytes.

HOW CAN YOU STOP COOKIES FROM BEING PASSED?

Here are three methods you can use to stop servers from delivering cookies to your PC:

1. One line of defense is to set Navigator so that it notifies you before a cookie is passed. Click on the **Options|Network Preferences** menu and then click on the tab labeled **Protocols**. Next, click on the box labeled "Show an Alert Before Accepting a Cookie."

2. A second option is to leave this box unchecked and then act to prevent servers from passing information to your PC. You do it by deleting all of the text in the *cookies.txt* file below the line that reads: "This is a generated file! Do not edit." Although the cookie file says, "Do not edit," there is nothing to stop you from doing this. Next, make the *cookies.txt* file *read only*. This will prevent others from writing information to that file. In Windows, follow these steps:

   a. Go to your MAIN Program Group and double-click on the File Manager icon. (In Windows 95, open Windows Explorer.)

   b. Find the Netscape folder and click on it once. (In Windows 95, the *cookies.txt* file may be in the C:\Program Files\Netscape\Navigator folder.)

   c. Look at the right side of your screen and find the *cookies.txt* file. Click on it once.

   d. Next go to the menu bar at the top of your screen and click on the word **File** and then choose **Properties**

e. In the Properties for COOKIES.TXT window, click on the box labeled **Read Only**. Then click on **OK**.

There is one problem with this option. Although the server cannot write information to your PC's hard disk, the server still can look at the cookie information while it is stored in RAM if your browser is open. To close up this security hole, you need a third option.

3. The third option is to use a utility program specifically designed to control cookies. PGPcookie.cutter can be downloaded from Pretty Good Privacy, Inc.'s site at *www.pgp.com* and sells for $19.95. Other cookie controllers can be found on Web sites featuring software, such as *www8.zdnet.com*. Search on names such as *Cookie Cruncher*, *CookieMaster*, and *Cookie Cutter*.

What Are E-Mail Bombs?

E-mail bombs, or "E-Bombs" occur when someone subscribes you to thousands of mailing lists. This leads to thousands of unwanted e-mail messages being sent to your mailbox. It is a major nuisance to both your Internet service provider and to you if you get stuck on the receiving end.

DOING BUSINESS ONLINE

Librarians and teachers doing business on the Internet should be concerned that vendors operate secure transactions and should know how their security is handled. There are many companies working on the development of secure transaction systems. For example, Microsoft is developing PCT (Private Communications Technology) and IBM is developing iKP (internet Keyed Payment).

What Is SSL?

Netscape Communications Corporation designed the SSL protocol (Secure Sockets Layer) to provide secure communications on the Internet. SSL works by using something called a *secure socket*, or port for transferring the information between servers and browsers. In this instance, a *port* is not a physical connection on the back of a computer; it is a software address. Sensitive information, such as credit card data, flowing in and out of this port is encrypted.

SSL also checks to see that the information flowing between your browser and the server does not get changed during transmission. Before you can take advantage of SSL, you must have a browser that supports SSL and the server you connect to must also support SSL.

What Is S-HTTP?

S-HTTP (Secure HyperText Transfer Protocol) is a protocol that works at the application level, encrypting the HTML (HyperText Markup Language) page itself. S-

---

Where to Get More Information on SSL

Join the ssl-talk mailing list to learn more about secure sockets layer. To join, send the word **subscribe** in the body of an e-mail message to *ssl-talk-request@netscape.com*. Leave the subject line blank.

HTTP was originally developed by Enterprise Integration Technologies in cooperation with RSA Data Security and the National Center for Supercomputing Applications. S-HTTP uses encryption to protect data being transferred between your Web browser and the vendor's Web server. In order for S-HTTP to work on your end of the connection, you need to have a browser that supports S-HTTP. At present Internet Explorer, Netscape, and SPRY Mosaic fall into this category.

More Information on S-HTTP

Interested in learning more about S-HTTP? The *shttp-talk* mailing list is the place to go to ask questions, air concerns, talk about specifications and documentation. Here's how to join: Send e-mail to *shttp-talk-request@ OpenMarket.com*. In the body of the message, type **subscribe**

How Do You Know If You Are Connecting to a Secure Site?

In Netscape 3.0, if you look under **Options|Security Preferences|General**, you see a Security Alerts section with check boxes. Depending on your choices, you can determine whether you receive a popup alert when connecting to a secure server, leaving a secure server, viewing a document with a mixed security status, or submitting a form that is insecure. If a check box is not checked, the popup alert does not appear.

Each time you view a popup alert, you can uncheck the **Show This Alert Next Time** check box.

The Enable SSL v2 and Enable SSL v3 check boxes determine whether you enable the security features of SSL version 2 and SSL version 3. Both check boxes are checked by default. When you click on the **Configure** button, you can enable the various ciphers associated with each version. When SSL is activated, the small broken key icon located in the lower left corner of the Navigator 3.0 window becomes whole and the shading behind the key turns dark blue. To see how this works (assuming that you have SSL enabled), open the **Help** menu in Netscape Navigator and click **On Security**. Now click on the link located in the left panel labeled **Download 128–bit Navigator**. From this point forward, the information that you send and receive is encrypted. The key is whole and the URL now begins with *https://*, which means you are connected with a secure document.

Netscape Communicator 4.0 displays an image of a padlock that opens and closes in the lower left corner of the screen. When you connect to *https://www.netvision.net.il/*, for example, the padlock closes and the background color turns yellow. This signifies that the data transferred is in an encrypted state.

To view the site's certificate, click once on the locked padlock and then click on the button labeled **View Certificate.** The *certificate* identifies the individual or organization associated with the Web page you are viewing.

WHAT IS A SITE CERTIFICATE?

When you click on the **View Certificate** button, you are presented with a certificate that belongs to *www.netvision.net.il.* This *site certificate* ensures that the information you send to this site goes where it is supposed to and that the connection is secure. Netscape can ensure a secure connection only with a server that holds a digital certificate from one of the certificate authorities listed in your preferences.

HOW DO YOU KNOW WHICH CERTIFICATE AUTHORITIES ARE RECOGNIZED BY NETSCAPE?

Certificates are not free. Both sites and individuals purchase certificates from independent authorities, such as VeriSign (*www.verisign.com*). To see a complete list of certificate authorities recognized by Netscape, click on the padlock in the lower left corner of your screen. In the next window that appears, there is a panel on the left side of the screen with a heading named **Certificates.** Click on the subheading **Signers.** This presents a list of certificate authorities.

Internet Security Resource Center

CERT Coordination Center (*www.cert.org* or *ftp.cert.org*) was formed in 1988 to serve as a focal point for the computer security concerns of Internet users.

How Safe Are SSL Messages?

In an experiment conducted in July 1995, a computerist sent an encrypted message to Netscape and challenged the hacking community to see whether they could crack the encrypted message. It took Damien Doligez, a French researcher using 112 workstations, eight days to crack the message. Later, Andrew Twyman of MIT accomplished the same feat in about the same time on a single $83,000 graphics computer from Integrated Computing Engines (ICE).

The message was encrypted with the International version 40–bit encryption key. You can tell which version you have running on your PC by opening the **Help** menu and clicking on **About Netscape.** Browsers supporting the 128–bit key state that they support U.S. security with RSA Public Key Cryptography. The 40–bit versions state that they support International security with RSA Public Key Cryptography.

Using SSL and SHTTP to encrypt sensitive data does not protect you from interlopers. There are JavaScript holes that make it possible for malicious Web site designers to pull data out of your Web browser form before it gets scrambled and sent across the Net.

> ## Web-related Security Issues
>
> Rutgers' Web Security Site at *http://www-ns.rutgers.edu/ www-security/index.html* connects you to security information relating to HTTP, HTML, and Web-related software and protocols. The WWW Security site is maintained by the Rutgers University Network Services www-security team. This team of specialists also manages the www-security mailing list, which is archived at *www-ns.rutgers.edu/ www-security/archives/index.html.* You can go to this site and browse through hundreds of security-related messages, which can be sorted by date, thread, author, or subject.

What Is SET?

SET, which stands for *Secure Electronic Transaction,* is an emerging security standard developed jointly by Visa and MasterCard. SET focuses on developing trust between the buyers, sellers, and financial institutions involved with credit card transactions. SET requires that they all get digital certificates—digital IDs verifying their identity. Many individuals already send their credit card numbers over the Net to buy books. They usually do it with a Secure Sockets Layer (SSL) connection, which secures the pathway between the user and the merchant. SET would secure the data, too. Various certificate authorities will be supporting SET digital certificates including VeriSign, U.S. Postal Service, Entrust, and CyberTrust, to name a few.

WHAT IS JAVA AND JAVASCRIPT?

Java is a programming language developed by Sun Microsystems. It is used to create mini-applications known as *applets*, which are stored on Web servers. Browsers that support Java, that is to say, they support the <APPLET> tag in HTML documents, download Java applications and run them.

JavaScript is an interpreted language (not compiled) and designed for controlling the Netscape browser. For example, it can manipulate your browser's settings and open and close windows. JavaScript is also object oriented, which means it can create reusable objects, such as dialog boxes and windows.

DOES JAVA POSE A SECURITY RISK?

Java poses a potential risk because the applets run on your PC instead of on the server. Java does have some built-in safety features, but unfortunately security holes do exist. Java's security is built around a sandbox model. The sandbox is a restrictive area in which Java applets operate. While in the sandbox, an applet can't perform unauthorized system functions, such as read and write from disks or allocate memory. Some software developers find this environment to be too restrictive so subsequent versions of the Java Development Kit have started supporting digital signatures. Now, if an applet carries a signature, it may be able to leave the sandbox and enter another domain in your system.

To be on the safe side, turn off your Java feature unless you are sure the site you are visiting is safe. You shut it off under the **Netscape Security Preferences** menu. If you do download an applet and it behaves oddly, close down your browser completely and then restart it. To learn more about Java security, check out the Java Security FAQ at *java.sun.com/sfaq/*.

WHAT ARE "HOSTILE APPLETS"?

Java applets that are designed to create malicious acts, such as denial of service attacks, are known as *hostile applets*. *Denial of service* attacks are a fairly new computer crime. A denial of service attack occurs when a perpetrator bombards a particular computer with traffic, tying up its resources. Attacks can be launched against service providers on the Internet halting services to thousands of users, or attacks can be launched on a single PC.

You can visit various sites on the Web that play host to hostile applets. For example, if you go to *www.cyber.com/mirror/mladue/HostileApplets.html* and click on the applet described as, " . . . a bear that insists on marching to the beat of a different drummer," you will hear what sounds like a kettle drum glissando repeated over and over, ad infinitum. The only way to stop it is to close your browser. Other hostile applets will make your browser hang or use up so many system resources, your PC hangs. Explore at your own risk.

> ### Computer Security Information
>
> Computer Security Information - The National Institutes of Health Web site maintains a comprehensive list of security related resources at *www.alw.nih.gov/Security/security.html*. From this site, you can link to dozens of newsgroups that are devoted to security issues ranging from encryption to viruses. You also can find links to electronic magazines and newsletters, mailing lists, FAQs, RFCs, software, other Web sites, documents, and advisories.

DISCOVERING SECURITY HOLES

In the early summer of 1997, this headline came shooting across the Net: "Another hole poked in Communicator." I had just finished installing the Communicator software suite when this news item appeared on *www.news.com*. It was the fourth security hole found in Navigator 4.0 since it was first shipped in June 1997. Of the various bugs that have been discovered, the most threatening is one that allows Web designers to place applets on your hard drive which could in turn track your whereabouts on the Web and read what you keyed into your browser, such as credit card information.

Earlier JavaScript bugs similar to this one affected Microsoft's Internet Explorer as well. More recent problems, also associated with JavaScript, have occurred in stand-alone browsers along with the browser included in the Communicator 4.02 suite. This is life on the Net. Developers are under a lot of pressure to release new versions of their software. There is not enough time to test programs thoroughly for security flaws.

Your best line of defense against security holes in newly released software is to follow these steps:

1. When buying your first browser, get the newest release available.
2. Budget for upgrades every six months. Running up-to-date browsers can protect you against known attacks.
3. Stay current with the latest news about security flaws. Schedule a weekly visit to *www.news.com*.
4. Download patches when they are made available.

Bounty for Bugs?

Netscape Communications sponsors a program called Bugs Bounty that offers a T-shirt and $1,000 to anyone who discovers a security glitch in their software.

ARE THERE SECURITY RISKS ASSOCIATED WITH ActiveX?

Microsoft Corporation's ActiveX is a proprietary technology used to present Web pages and it is designed to work hand-in-hand with Internet Explorer. If you are not using Internet Explorer, you won't benefit from the full functionality of pages that are designed using ActiveX. For example, to view scrolling marquees, you would need an ActiveX control designed to view scrolling marquees. Internet Explorer version 3.0 and later have that capability. If you were using Netscape, you could not view the object unless you installed a plug-in that supports ActiveX.

It is possible, too, that in the future ActiveX extensions may become part of the HTML standards.

ActiveX is a security risk because it implements a technology that enables the downloading of programs to your hard drive. It is possible for a programmer to create a program that contains malicious code—code that destroys data on your hard drive, for example. To counter this risk, Microsoft began incorporating digital signatures into ActiveX controls. These digital signatures, or "certificates," use Microsoft Authenticode technology and allow you to verify who created the control and assess whether they are a reliable source. Authenticode uses a two-key encryption system—a private key to generate the signature and a public key, which is available to the world, to validate the signature.

Independent certificate authorities, such as VeriSign, issue the digital signatures. Software developers have to pass a screening process before being issued a certificate.

You might be wondering what prevents a software publisher from signing malicious code? How many programmers will attach a digital signature to their code? And how many individuals will refuse to accept a control when a warning box pops up on the screen telling you in advance that the control is unsigned? What if you assume that a particular ActiveX developer is reliable and then discover that their ActiveX control damages your system? It becomes apparent that ActiveX is more of an authentication system and less of a security model.

The security problems associated with ActiveX controls were made apparent when, in 1997, a group of German hackers known as The Chaos Computer Club demonstrated a malicious ActiveX component. (See "ActiveX

Used as Hacking Tool," by Nick Wingfield at *www.news. com/News/Item/0,4,7761,4000.html.*) In a national broadcast appearance, the Club demonstrated an ActiveX control that was capable of taking money from one bank account and depositing it into another without using a personal identification number (PIN). If you are concerned about the security of data stored on a PC running Internet Explorer, simply disable the ActiveX support in that PC's browser.

ActiveX Technology

To learn more about ActiveX, visit *www.microsoft.com/ activex/.* The security features of ActiveX are addressed at *www.microsoft.com/security/.*

HOW TO HIDE YOUR IDENTITY ON THE NET

Most everyone likes some level of privacy in his or her life, and that includes online life. Programs such as file shredders and encryptors, introduced in Chapter 7, help you keep the contents of your files secure. In this section, you learn how to remain anonymous when sending e-mail by using anonymous remailers. Only in very rare instances would you use this procedure in the context of your job. For example, there may be an instance where you would want to respond to a newsgroup or mailing list posting anonymously rather than as an official spokesperson for your school or library. Other than in this case, it is beneficial at least to understand how the process works and know that others may be using it all around you.

This section also introduces you to Web anonymizers. These services operate on the same principle that an anonymous remailer operates, except that they help you surf the Web anonymously.

What Is an Anonymous Remailer?

An *anonymous remailer* is an anonymous server on the Net that operates as a middleman between you and the individuals with whom you exchange e-mail. The server assigns you a unique ID and return address, which is used to maintain your anonymity. The popularity of anonymous remailers is exemplified by the recent closing down of one of the most popular services on the Net, Johan Helsingius's *Anon.penet.fi* in Finland. Increasing workload (partly from spammers sending junk mail) and questions about the legality of anonymous e-mail in Finland were the reasons stated for closing down the service. For more details, see *www.penet.fi/*. At the time *Anon.penet.fi* closed, it had just under 700,000 registered users and was handling about 10,000 messages a day.

A specialized type of remailer called a *cypherpunk remailer* does not use an anonymous ID and return address. Cypherpunk remailers strip the header information off your e-mail before sending it to the recipient. The ability to trace the source of your message may vary depending on the mail programs being used on your end and the recipient's end.

How Does an Anonymous Remailer Work?

Anonymous remailers do one of two things:

1. They send your message without any trace of who you are or what your address is, or
2. They assign you an anonymous ID and address that other people use to send you mail. The remailer intercepts the message and forwards it onto your real address.

Another, yet not always secure method of sending anonymous messages is to use a form in an HTML document. The unsecured WWW remailers send your messages to WWW server unencrypted. Anyone on the network between you and the recipient can determine your identity and the content of your message. One such service is The Replay Remailer at *www.replay.com/remailer/anon.html*. You can access OzEmail, a more secure Java-based WWW remailer, at *www.ozemail.com.au/~geoffk/anon/anon.html*.

Where Can I Learn More about Anonymous Remailers?

To learn more about the principles behind anonymous remailers, check out Andre Bacard's *Non-technical Anonymous Remailer FAQ*. You can find a copy at *www.well.com/user/abacard/remail.html*. For an updated list of reliable remailers, refer to Raph Levin's *Remailer List* at *www.cs.berkeley.edu/~raph/remailer-list.html*.

> **Resource Tip**
>
> The Library of Congress Internet Resource Page - The Library of Congress maintains a meta site on Internet security at *lcweb.loc.gov/global/internet/security.html*. From here, you can link to resource pages with information on security alerts, RFCs, papers on Internet security, UNIX security tools, security-related mailing lists and newsgroups, cryptography, viruses, and more.

What Is the Anonymizer and How Does It Work?

Have you ever linked to a Web page where you were met with a statement announcing the name of your host and what type of Web browser you are using? Under special circumstances, the server also may be able to determine your name and e-mail address. If you see this as a violation of your privacy, you may want to consider using The Anonymizer, written by Justin Boyan at Carnegie Mellon University. The Anonymizer, located at *www.anonymizer.com/*, is a service that enables you to surf the Web without revealing your identity to the sites you visit.

Before you can use The Anonymizer, you must go to The Anonymizer site on the Web and register. You can register for a free trial version or set up an Anonymizer account. The paid version runs faster than the unlimited, free Anonymizer trial version.

The Anonymizer works like this: When you want to visit *www.somebody.com*, for example, you type in The Anonymizer's address first (in the URL field), and then follow it with the URL to which you want to connect. In this example, the full address would be *http:// www.anonymizer.com:8080/http://www.somebody.com/*. (Port 8080 is used for the free, unlimited trial versions and port 8040 is used with The Anonymizer subscriptions.) The Anonymizer acts as an intermediary by connecting to the site you specified. It retrieves the document *www.somebody.com* and rewrites all the links so they point back to *www.anonymizer.com*. It also removes any unsecured elements, such as Java and JavaScript.

When you surf using The Anonymizer, document URLs will have the prefix *http://www.anonymizer.com:8040* or *http://www.anonymizer.com:8080;* The Anonymizer inserts a control bar at the beginning and end of the document with buttons that read: **open anonymous, bug report,** and **anonymizer help;** and the title of the document has the word "Anonymized" attached to it.

The World Wide Web Security FAQ
Maintained by Lincoln D. Stein

Refer to this document for answers to questions relating to Web server security. This FAQ also includes a short section on Web browser security. You can find a copy of this FAQ at *www-genome.wi.mit.edu/WWW/faqs/*.

HOW TO MAKE NETSCAPE NAVIGATOR SECURE

In this last section, I show you how you can lock down Netscape Navigator using Borland's Resource Workshop. There are other options available as well, such as IKIOSK. Hyper Technologies, Inc., made an agreement with CARL Corporation to market their security software IKIOSK with Everybody's Menu Builder. (See Chapter 5 for details on Everybody's Menu Builder.)

IKIOSK can be used to disable functions such as Minimize and Maximize; restrict access to desktop and File Manager; and it can control which menu items are available.

To learn more about IKIOSK, go to CARL Corporation's site at *www.carl.org/emb/ikiosk.html.*

Microsoft Security Information and Code Updates

Go to *www.microsoft.com/ie/security/update.htm* for Internet-related security issues that affect users of Microsoft products.

LOCKING DOWN NETSCAPE 3.0 WITH A RESOURCE EDITOR

In computerese, *resource data* is the data that defines what you see in a Windows program—the cursor, toolbars, and menus, etc. Resources make it easy for you to switch from one function to another in Windows. A *resource editor* is a specialized utility that enables you to edit resources. That is to say, it helps you create and edit dialog boxes and pop-up menus; and design icons and cursors, etc.

Resource Workshop 4.5 by Borland International is the resource editor I use in this section to illustrate how to gray-out menu items. You can obtain a copy of this application by contacting Borland's sales department at (800) 932–9994. The cost is $69.95 plus $5.00 for shipping and handling.

How to Edit Netscape 3.0 Menus

Here are the steps to follow to make Netscape secure by graying-out menu items.

1. Begin by making a backup copy of *netscape.exe*. You could name it something like *scapebkp.exe* and store it in the same directory as the copy you are about to modify. These editors are powerful utilities and you may make a mistake that renders Netscape useless. It is also important to keep a backup for those occasions when you want to run the unaltered version.

2. Resource Workshop has four icons in its program group. Double-click on the icon labeled **Resource Workshop**. Once it is open, choose **File|Open Project**.

3. Enter the path and file name in the dialog box. In this example, I stored a copy of *netscape.exe* in the C:\TEMP directory, so I entered C:\TEMP*netscape. exe* and then clicked **OK**. This action takes *netscape.exe*, which is an executable program, and decompiles it. A window opens with **netscape.exe** written on the title bar.

4. Maximize the window and scroll down until you find **MENU** as shown in Figure 8–1. Click on the **2** to open the editing dialog box for Menu 2. Menu 2 enables you to edit Netscape's main menus including File, Edit, View, Go, Bookmarks, Options, Directory, Windows, and Help. From this point, you take slightly different paths, depending on which menu you are editing. In this exercise, you will be editing three menu items that create the most problems on public-access PCs running Netscape 2.0 and 3.0:

   - **File|Mail Document** - This allows patrons to attempt sending e-mail even if the e-mail service is not available.
   - **File|Open File** - This makes it easy for patrons to view the hard drive and open files.
   - **Options/General Preferences** - This enables patrons to change Netscape's appearance.
   - **Options/Save Options** - This makes it possible for patrons to change menu options and then save them. (This menu item exists only in version 2.0.)

How to Edit the Mail Document Menu

1. Choose the pull-down menu labeled **Resource** and click on **Edit**.
2. Look in the lower, right corner of the screen. Find the **MENUITEM-Ma&il Document** choice and highlight it by clicking on it once.
3. Now go to the section labeled **Initial state** on the left side of the screen. Notice that the **Enabled** checkbox has a mark in it. To disable it, you have two choices:

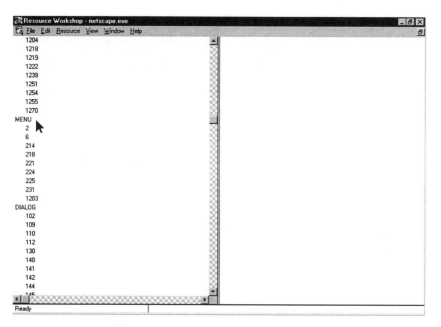

Figure 8–1: Window for editing menus

You can either check **Disable** or **Grayed**. For this exercise, choose **Grayed** as shown in Figure 8–2. Now when you run the modified version of Netscape, the **File|Mail Document** menu will be grayed-out.

How to Edit the Open File Menu

1. Choose the pull-down menu labeled **Resource** and click on **Edit**.
2. Look in the lower, right corner of the screen. Find the **MENUITEM-Open &File** choice and highlight it by clicking on it once.
3. Now go to the section labeled **Initial state** on the left side of the screen. Disable the **Open File** menu item by clicking on **Grayed**.

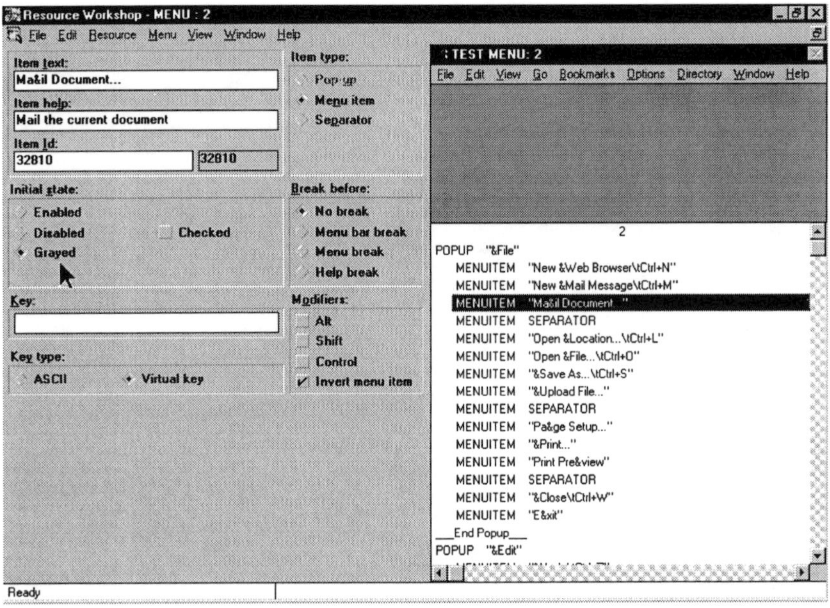

Figure 8–2: Menu items are grayed-out by clicking on the Grayed checkbox

How to Edit the Options|Preferences Menu

1. Choose the pull-down menu labeled **Resource** and click on **Edit**.
2. Look in the lower, right corner of the screen. Find the **MENUITEM-Open &File** choice and highlight it by clicking on it once.
3. Now go to the section labeled **Initial state** on the left side of the screen. Disable the **Open File** menu item by clicking on **Grayed**.

How to Edit the Options|Save Options Menu

1. Choose the pull-down menu labeled **Resource** and click on **Edit**.

2. Look in the lower, right corner of the screen. Find the **MENUITEM-&Save Options** choice and highlight it by clicking on it once.

3. Now go to the section labeled **Initial state** on the left side of the screen. Disable the **Save Options** menu item by clicking on **Grayed**.

How to Edit Netscape 3.0 Dialog Boxes

In the next exercise, you will be editing the **Unknown File Type** dialog box. Save your project and close the **MENU 2** window from the previous exercise by double-clicking on the control box (close button) in the upper left-hand corner of the window. Be careful not to close Resource Workshop. If you do, simply restart Resource Workshop and repeat the first three steps in the first exercise.

Follow these steps to edit the **Unknown File Type** dialog box and the **Send Mail/Post News** dialog box:

1. First, find the word **DIALOG** on the left side of the screen. It should be just below the **MENU** section. Scroll down until you find **142**. Highlight **142** and then click on the **Resource** menu and choose **Edit**. This will bring up the image shown in Figure 8–3.

2. Double-click on the button labeled **Pick Application** to open a new dialog box shown in Figure 8–4. Look on the left side of the screen for a section labeled **Attributes**. Click on the box labeled **Disabled** and then click on **OK**.

3. Repeat step 2, only this time use the button labeled **Save File**.

4. Close the current window by double-clicking on the

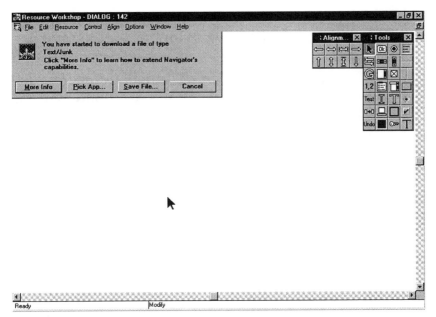

Figure 8–3: Preparing to edit the dialog box

close button in the upper left corner of the resource
screen. Again, be careful not to close Resource Workshop, which is the close button in the topmost upper left corner of the screen.

5. Next, edit the **Send Mail|Post News dialog** by scroll-
ing through choices on the left side of the screen until you come to number **141** under the word
DIALOG. Highlight the number **141** and then click
on the **Resource** menu and choose **Edit.** This will
bring up the image shown in Figure 8–5.

6. Double-click on the **Send** button at the bottom of the
screen and then disable it as you did the **Choose Application** button in step 2 above. This prevents you
from accessing the e-mail system while you are in
Usenet News.

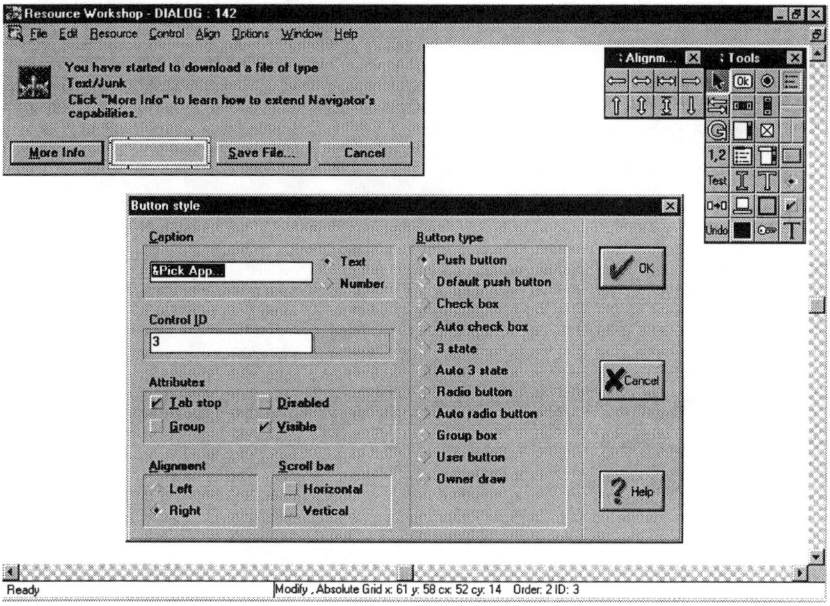

Figure 8–4: Editing screen for disabling the Pick Application **button**

7. Now go to the **File** menu and chose **Save Project** and then click on **Exit**.

8. The last step is to run *netscape.exe* and test your work. If everything is a go, you are all set to run the new edited version of Netscape on your public-access PCs. Remember, if something went wrong during the editing process, you always have the original executible file to fall back on.

Preventing Netscape from Displaying Local Files

If you enter the URL identifier **file:///** in Netscape's **Go to:** or **Location:** box you can display file directories on your

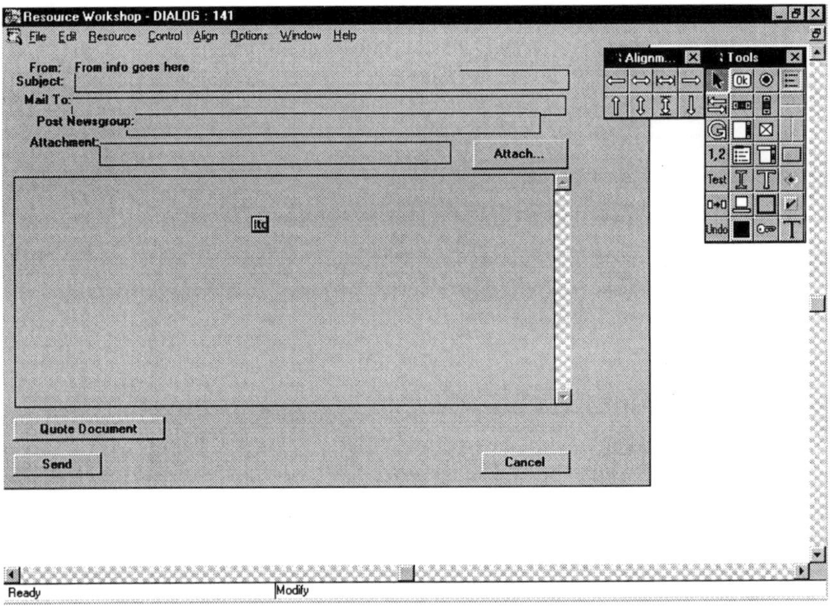

Figure 8–5: Editing the Send Mail|Post News **dialog box**

local disk drive. For example, if you enter **file:///C/** in the Location: box and press ENTER, your browser will list the root directory of your C drive. To list the contents of a floppy disk in the A drive, enter **file:///a/**. The 16–bit version of Netscape does not show Hidden files, but the 32–bit version does.

Hackers can gain a better understanding of your security setup if they have access to certain files, such as *config.sys* and *autoexec.bat*. If they cannot access a text editor to view these files, they might try using Netscape as a backdoor by typing **file:///C/** in the Location: box. Next, they would scroll through your files and directories until they found the file names they were interested in. Double-clicking on the file name pulls the file into the Netscape window for viewing.

You can prevent hackers from using Netscape to access local files by editing *netscape.exe* by using HEXpert (see Figure 8–6). HEXpert, a shareware program included on the CD-ROM that accompanies this book, enables you to search and edit binary data. (Look for the file named *hxp3010.zip* located in the EDITOR directory.) Follow these steps to restrict access to the **file:///** identifier. In this exercise, I show you how to edit the 32–bit version of Netscape Communicator 4.0.

1. Open HEXpert and specify which file you want to edit. Make a backup copy of *netscape.exe* before you begin. That way if you make a mistake you cannot undo, you still have a copy of the original *.exe* file.

2. When you first open *netscape.exe*, the screen shown in Figure 8–6 is displayed. Press ALT+S to search for the text string **file**. Continue to press ALT+N to find each subsequent occurrence of **file**. After about 66 hits (HEXpert also stops on substrings, such as Pro-**file**), you come to the section shown in Figure 8–7.

3. Notice in Figure 8–7 that HEXpert presents its data in three different regions. The region on the far left shows the offset in hex of each line of data. The occurrence of the word **file** I was looking for came on line **00365970**. This address is only accurate for the version of Netscape that I am editing. If you are editing Netscape version 2.01, for example, this occurrence of the word **file** would be found at a different address. The middle region in the HEXpert screen is the hexadecimal representation of the data. The furthest region to the right displays the data in plain ASCII text. This is the column you edit.

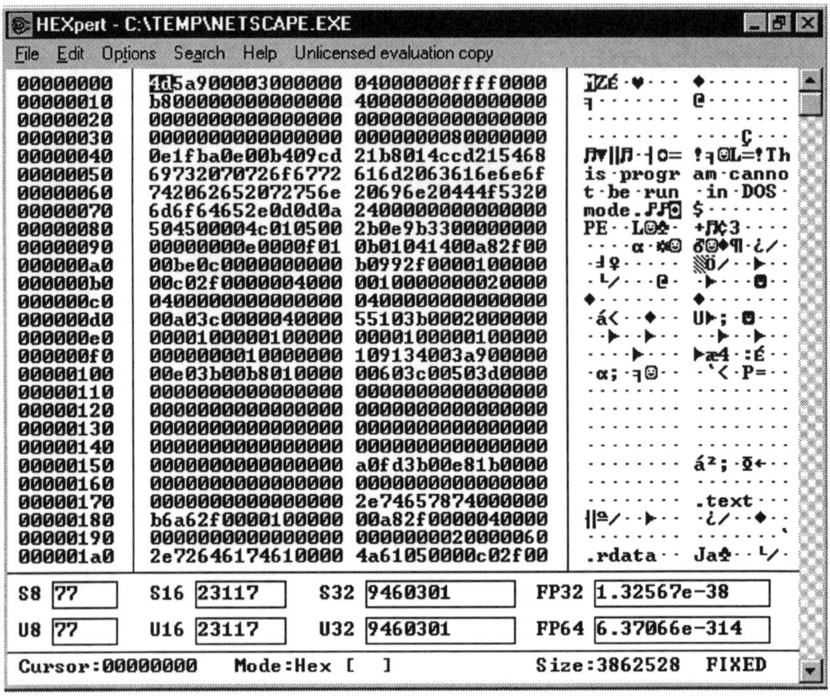

Figure 8–6: HEXpert editor's view of netscape.exe

4. Align the cursor so that it is on the "e" in the word "file." Next, press ALT+M to toggle the edit mode to ASCII. Look again at Figure 8–7 and note the **Mode:ASC [ ]** located at the bottom of the screen. This is the state in which you want the editor before editing the word **file.** Replace the letter "e" with another letter, for example, "x" (without the quotation marks). Now save the file by clicking on the **File** pulldown menu and choosing **Save.**

```
HEXpert - C:\PROGRA~1\NETSCAPE\COMMUN~1\PROGRAM\NETSCAP.EXE
File  Edit  Options  Search  Help  Unlicensed evaluation copy
00365930  72792d66696c652d  313e000025692200   ry-file- 1>··%i"·
00365940  2056495349545f43  4f554e543d220000   ·UISIT_C OUNT="··
00365950  2046495253545f56  495349543d220000   ·FIRST_U ISIT="··
00365960  6e6574776f726b2e  656e61626c655572   network. enableUr
00365970  6c4d617463680000  3a2f2f0055696c65   lMatch·· ://·file
00365980  3a0000006674703a  2f2f6674702e0000   :··ftp: //ftp.··
00365990  6674702e00000000  687474703a2f2f77   ftp.···· http://w
003659a0  77772e007777772e  0000000000000000   ww.·www. ········
003659b0  000000004e535f48  4953544f52595f4c   ····NS_H ISTORY_L
003659c0  494d495400000000  66696c653a2f2f2f   IMIT···· fil5:///
003659d0  556e7469746c6564  0000000061626f75   Untitled ····abou
003659e0  743a656469746669  6c656e6577000000   t:editfi lenew···
003659f0  4e65746361737465  725f53656c656374   Netcaste r_Select
00365a00  6f72546162000000  0000000000000000   orTab··· ········
00365a10  000000006c6d2d71  756575652d6d6f6e   ····lm-q ueue-mon
00365a20  69746f7200000000  6d6f6363686612d6576   itor···· mocha-ev
00365a30  656e742d71756575  650000006d6f6368   ent-queu e···moch
00365a40  612d737461636b2d  71756575652d2564   a-stack- queue-%d
00365a50  0000000050726566  436f6e6669672e67   ····Pref Config.g
00365a60  65745f757365725f  7072656628707265   et_user_ pref(pre
00365a70  66732e2573290000  4170706c65744172   fs.%s)·· AppletAr
00365a80  7261790000000000  50937600ff070000   ray····· Pov·····
00365a90  0000000000000000  0000000000000000   ········ ········

S8  102      S16 26982     S32 1701603686    FP32 6.97764e+22
U8  102      U16 26982     U32 1701603686    FP64 1.23916e-312
Cursor:0036597c    Mode:ASC [ ]              Size:3862528   FIXED
```

Figure 8-7: The section of netscape.exe illustrating the text surrounding the word file

5. Restart Netscape and test your change. When you attempt to display the root directory using the URL file:///Cl/, you should get an error message similar to the one shown in Figure 8-8. In Netscape Communicator 4.0, it is possible to regain access to the root directory by entering the altered form file:///cl/ in the Location: box.

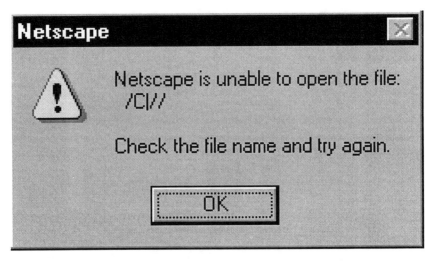

Figure 8–8: Error message that displays when trying to access the disabled URL file:///c|/

Appendix

The *Securing PCs and Data* Software Toolbox

This appendix describes the programs included with the CD-ROM that accompanies this book. As you try out the various shareware, freeware, and demo programs, you will be installing and deleting a lot of software. Make sure that you remove each application completely when you are finished with it so you do not clutter your system with unnecessary DLL files and Registry entries, etc.

Run uninstall programs when they are available. If you are not given the uninstall option, or uninstall does not do a complete job, try using Rosenthal UnInstall. Uninstall tracks changes to your system files and the Win95 Registry files *SYSTEM.DAT* and *USER.DAT*. UnInstall runs in DOS, Win3.x and Win95. You can find a copy on the Web at *slonet.org/~doren/*.

HOW ARE THE APPLICATIONS ORGANIZED?

The CD-ROM contains a *readme.txt* file, which is an abbreviated, plain ASCII text version of this document. All of the software included on the CD-ROM is contained in these ten directories:

ACCESS - Access control utilities
AV - Anti-virus software
CRYPTO - Cryptography-related applications
DIGITAL - Digital signatures
EDITOR - Viewing and editing in hex
F_BKUP - File back-up
F_SHRDNG - File shredding
MISC - Miscellaneous utilities
PSSWRD - Password management utilities
TEXT - Text files

Within each of these directories are subdirectories that contain one application each. For example, the ACCESS directory contains eight applications and eight corresponding subdirectories. Each subdirectory is named after the file it contains, minus the three-letter extension. For example, the subdirectory **bdswinu** contains *bdswinu.exe*; the subdirectory **lockf15** contains *lockf15.zip*, and so on.

Files that are compressed and archived with PKZIP are presented in both their zipped and unzipped state. For example, when you view the contents of the **lockf15** subdirectory, you will see *lockf15.zip* and you will see 23 other files, which are *lockf15.zip* after it has been unarchived and uncompressed. Both the zipped and unzipped versions of files are presented for two reasons:

1. You can copy the original zipped application to your hard drive if you wish;
2. The zip file has been unzipped for you in case you don't have your own copy of PKUNZIP. This enables you to view the *readme.txt* and *install.txt* files right away with a text editor, such as Notepad. You can then go right to work installing the program by double-clicking on the *setup.exe* if one exists.

Most of the applications require you to run a setup program. Some directories, however, contain nothing more than a single executable file or a single self-extracting file.

FILE DESCRIPTIONS

In this section, I present descriptions of all the files contained on the CD-ROM and list where you can find the latest versions of each application on the Web.

Directory Name: ACCESS
Contents: Access Control Utilities

BDSWINU.EXE (168KB) WinU 3.2 from Bardon Data Systems is a shareware menu system for Windows 95. WinU features automatic time limits, multiple password-protected desktops, three levels of security control, and several configuration options. WinU enables you to use any image you choose, such as your library or school building, as wallpaper behind WinU's menu buttons. You can download the latest version of WinU from Bardon Data Systems' Web site at *www.bardon.com*.

LOCKF15.ZIP (2,100KB) Lockwk-Workstation Lock Pro 1.5ap shareware for Windows 95 locks down your computer completely so no one can access it while you are away. Even if your PC is rebooted, only those who know the password can get back in.

You can download the latest version from Lockwk-Workstation Lock Pro home page at *wibbleinc. home.ml.org.*

LOG32.ZIP (8KB) Win-Log 1.0 is a freeware Windows 95 utility that logs the use of Windows on your PC. For top security, the program remains hidden while it logs when and how many times your PC is used. You can get updates of the software from ///iNFiNiTY Software's home page at *www.griffin.co.uk/users/jcross/.*

PCSEC16.EXE (210KB) PC Security for Windows 95 demo from Tropical Software. Features include Program Manager control, file locking, system locking, keyboard monitoring, Window locking, intruder detection with alarm, password protection, and DES encryption. For the latest version, go to *www.tropsoft.com/pcsecwin/ index.htm.*

PCSEC32.EXE This is the Windows 3.1 version of PC Security from Tropical Software.

PPDEMO.EXE (1,100KB) Program Protector 2.2 demo for Windows 95 prevents unauthorized individuals from running programs on your Windows 95 PC. A password box is displayed before programs can be run. The registered version supports multiple usernames and passwords, a log file, and administration features. You can download the latest version of Program Protector from M Benadiba

Consulting's home page at *www.globalserver.net/ ~sberkovitz/mbconsulting/index.html.*

SL95ELS.EXE (840KB) This is the StopLight 95 ELS (Entry Level Security) security system from SafteyNet. It is just one in a family of products offered by SafteyNet that offers myriad access control and file-locking capabilities. This entry-level program for PCs and laptops supports several features including restricting access to programs, preventing changes to system settings, requiring login at bootup, and it is capable of recording user's activities.

SL95PC.EXE (1,033KB) StopLight 95 PC is a mid-level security system that includes the same features as StopLight 95 ELS plus it offers full-disk encryption, diskette security, boot protection, and advanced auditing capabilities.

SL95PRO.EXE (1,296KB) StopLight 95 Pro is the high-end security program with all of the features included in the ELS and PC versions, plus it offers real-time and manual data encryption. It also prevents breaking out of bootup and bypassing security by using a floppy disk, and it protects the hard disk drive from disk sector editing programs.

STORMW43.ZIP (1,071KB) StormWindows V.4.3 for Windows 95 is a shareware application that allows you to enable various types of desktop protection. Features include hiding desktop icons, disabling the DOS prompt, disabling restarting in DOS, preventing warm booting with CTRL-ALT-DEL, and more. You can get the latest release of StormWindows from Cetus Software Inc. at *www.cetussoft.com.*

ZAPIT22.EXE (685KB) Zap It! version 2.2 is a freeware application for individuals with highly sensitive documents or programs. Zap It! enables you to keep an updated list of the sensitive programs and files on your hard drive. In the event someone sees or uses your PC that shouldn't, Zap It! deletes all files in the list. Zap It! is published by Cripton Corporation at *www.cripton.com*.

Directory Name: AV
Contents: Anti-virus Software

BOOTMNDR.ZIP (109KB) Bootminder 2.0, created by Henk Hagedoorn, is an anti-virus program that helps prevent boot virus infection. Bootminder reminds you when you leave a floppy disk in your A: drive when closing down Windows.

The latest version of Bootminder can be found on the Freebyte! home page at *www.freebyte.com/freew1.htm*.

NAV9540.EXE (6,877KB) Norton AntiVirus (NAV) 4.0 for Windows 95 is the latest version of Symantec's virus-protection software. The application included on this CD-ROM is a full-featured "try before you buy" version.

Like other programs in its class, NAV helps protect against virus infection from floppy disks, e-mail attachments, networks, and the Internet. NAV 4.0 supports a new feature called LiveUpdate, which automatically updates your system with the latest virus signature files. LiveUpdate is set to visit Symantec's Web site once a week to download the latest signature files, which are free of charge. NAV also keeps you up-to-date by sending you e-mail updates informing you of the latest virus outbreaks.

NAV 4.0 is priced at $49.95 and you can order it online from Symantec's Web site at *www.symantec.com*, or by calling 800–441–7234, or 541–334–6054.

PC2TRIAL.EXE (4,800KB) PC-cillin II version 2.0 antivirus software is a trial version for Windows. You can order PC-Cillin II online or by calling (800) 932–5566. Features include a macro shield—a virus detector that detects known and unidentified new strains of macro viruses. To obtain the latest version available, go to TouchStone Software's Web site at *www.checkit.com/products/pcc2.htm*.

VDOC25.EXE (212KB) ViruSafe VDOC version 2.50 is a free copy of EliaShim, Inc.'s anti-virus scanner for removing Word and Excel macro viruses. VDOC is Office 97 and network compatible. You can download the latest version from the Web site located at *www.eliashim.com*.

VNPC95.EXE (2,337KB) VirusNet 4.01 demo scanner supports Windows 95, Windows 3.x, and DOS. VirusNet detects over 9,000 different viruses including Word macro viruses. You can find the newest version at SafetyNet's home page *safetynet.com/*. While you are at this site, you can also download an evaluation copy of their LAN anti-virus product called VirusNet LAN.

VS75.EXE (2,033KB) ViruSafe v7.5 is an anti-virus utility for DOS and Windows from EliaShim, Inc. This is a full working copy for evaluation. Get the latest updates at *www.eliashim.com*.

VS95V40.EXE (3,500KB) ViruSafe 95 version 4.0 antivirus for Windows 95 from EliaShim, Inc. This is a full working copy made available for evaluation. ViruSafe 95 provides protection for viruses that are both known and unknown. This version of ViruSafe 95 incorporates ViruSafe-WEB. This allows you to check for viruses when downloading files from the Web and FTP sites. Stay up-to-date with ViruSafe's latest products by checking into their site at *www.eliashim.com/*.

VSWEB40.EXE (1,064KB) ViruSafe-WEB version 4.0 is an anti-virus plugin for Web browsers from EliaShim, Inc. ViruSafe automatically scans every file downloaded from the Web. This is a free, full working copy. The latest version can be downloaded from *www.eliashim.com*.

Directory Name: CRYPTO
Contents: Encryption Software

COT32.EXE (315KB) Crypt-o-Text 32 for Windows 95 is an easy-to-use security program that enables you to scramble text in e-mail messages. Text is unscrambled with a password.
   Download the latest version from Savard Software at *www.owt.com/users/rsavard/software.html*.

CRYPTEXT.ZIP (83KB) Cryptext v2.41, developed by Nick Payne, is a freeware Windows 95 shell extension that features point and click encryption and decryption. The program uses a combination of SHA-1 and RC4 to encrypt files using a 160–bit key. Updates can be found on Payne's Web page at *www.pcug.org.au/~njpayne*.

CYCODE.ZIP (300KB) Cycode is a freeware Windows 95 encryption program that allows you to encode/decode text in files and e-mail messages. Updated versions of Cycode can be downloaded from Jameson Blandford's home page at *www.proimaging.com/jamie/.*

EIW95SHR.EXE (600KB) This is the shareware version of Encyrpt-It for Win95 developed by MaeDae Enterprises. The program is a secure file encryption program featuring an online manual and file shredding abilities. When you encrypt files, you can choose between various cryptosystems ranging from their own proprietary system to the more advanced 448–bit Blowfish and Data Encryption Standard (DES). For program updates, go to MaeDae's Web site at *www.maedae.com/encr95.html.*

FLLITE.EXE (7,671KB) File Lock 95 Lite is a shareware encryption program developed by D & L Computing. File Lock uses Standard and Enhanced encryption methods to protect personal files. Check D & L Computing's Web site at *www.dlcomputing.com* for updates.

FLOCK95.EXE (7,859KB) File Lock 95 Standard, also from D & L Computing, uses some additional encryption methods not found in File Lock 95 Lite. The product is designed for protecting business-related information. Look for updates at D & L Computing's Web site *www. dlcomputing.com.* Follow the links **Products|File Lock Series**.

FLW.EXE (2,834KB) File Lock Wizard for Windows 95 is the most user-friendly program in D & L Computing's File Lock series. It supports three encryption algorithms and four compression algorithms. Go to D & L Computing's Web site at *www.dlcomputing.com* for updates.

LK32V400.ZIP (385KB) Lock & Key is a Windows 95

shareware application that integrates PGP with Windows 95 Explorer interface. You can simply right-click on a file to encrypt it. Double-clicking on an encrypted file decrypts it. You can find updates of Lock & Key online at Walter E. Heindl's Web site *www.voicenet.com/~wheindl/ order.htm.*

MAILPG13.ZIP (145KB) MailPGP is a freeware program for Windows 95 that provides a friendly interface for Philip Zimmermann's Pretty Good Privacy (PGP). MailPGP enables you to encrypt and decrypt messages by dragging and dropping. It requires PGP 2.6.2 or later. For updates, go to the MailPGP home page at *www.students.tut.fi/~stv/ mailpgp/.*

SAFUS.EXE (1,615KB) Citadel Safstor is a product of Citadel Data Security. Citadel Safstor adds menu items to the context menu that is displayed when you right click on a file name. You are given the option to encrypt or decrypt the file you have selected. For the latest version of Citadel Safstor, go to Citadel Data Security's Web site at *www.cdsec.com/safstor.html.*

SECURE.ZIP (700KB) DataSafe is a Windows 95 Shareware data encryption package from Revelation Labs, Inc. DataSafe includes 40–bit DES and 40–bit Blowfish ciphers due to US export regulations. Registered shareware has complete 56–bit DES and 448–bit Blowfish cipher along with Triple DES cipher. Download the latest file encryption software from Revelation Labs at *www-eland.stanford.edu/~jmansell/RevLabs.*

XCRYPT.ZIP (285KB) XCrypt for Windows 95 is a front-end to PGP encryption. XCrypt works with any e-mail or word processing software. Version 1.02 of XCrypt requires PGP 2.6.2 or later. XCrypt Light is the freeware version of the program. You can download the latest version free from XCrypt's home page at *www.21x.com/xcrypt/*.

Directory Name: DIGITAL
Contents: Digital Signatures

ADDEMO.EXE (480KB) This is a demo movie that shows how the PenOp Acrobat plug-in can be used to sign an acrobat document. For updates, check PenOp's product information page at *www.penop.com/ver2/product.htm*.

PENOPW16.EXE (201KB) PenOp/View version 2.62 for Windows 3.x enables you to view PenOp's signature image, see the date and time it was signed, and check that the document hasn't been altered since signing. Updated versions are available at PenOp's Web site *www.penop. com*.

PENOPW32.EXE (308KB) This is the Windows 95/NT version of PenOp/View. Updates can be found at PenOp's Web site *www.penop.com*.

Directory Name: EDITOR
Contents: Viewing and editing in hex

HXP3010.ZIP (245KB) HEXpert for Windows Release 3.0 includes 16– and 32–bit versions. HEXpert is an editor that allows you to view and edit binary files in hex, octal, binary, decimal, and ASCII formats. With HEXpert you can edit, search, insert, or delete data in any of these formats. Chapter 8 shows you how to use HEXpert to disable features in Netscape 4.0. You can find the latest version of HEXpert on Matthew Woolsey's home page at *www.flash.net/~mwoolsey/hexpert.html*, or you can write to Woolsey at P.O. Box 832071, Richardson, TX 75083–2071.

Directory Name: F_ BKUP
Contents: File Back-up

LIFESAVR.ZIP (1,500KB) LifeSaver shareware backs up critical Windows 95 files. If you have problems because your configuration files have gotten corrupted and you can't fix them, LifeSaver can help you recover. Standard features include backing up and restoring as many as seven different configuration files including the registry. Additional features are made available to registered users. To download the latest version available, go to LifeSaver's home page at *members.aol.com/aeroblade/index.html*.

RESCUE99.ZIP (522KB) Rescue 95 is a shareware program for Windows 95 that backs up and restores your Windows 95 registry. The program includes a DOS-based rescue program in case Windows 95 doesn't start. Super Win Software maintains the latest version of WinRescue 95 at *superwin.com/rescue.htm*.

SETUP40.EXE (537KB) Second Copy 97 for Windows is a backup utility that helps you organize your backup requirements into separate profiles. Each profile has its own specifications including what files to copy, when to copy them, and where to place the backup copies. You can get the latest version of Second Copy 97 and the Windows 3.1

version (Second Copy 4.0) from Centered Systems' Web site at *www.centered.com*.

TRANSX95.EXE (227KB) Transfer 95 shareware helps you transfer, copy, upgrade, and back up your Windows 95 operating system. The product is useful when you are backing up your hard drive to removable media, such as a Zip or Jaz drive. You can find the latest version of this utility on ITS Systems' home page at *www.itechs-systems.com*.

Directory Name: F_SHRDNG
Contents: File Shredding

DEL121.ZIP (65KB) Michael Paul Johnson's DELETE offers enhancements to the DEL and ERASE DOS commands. DELETE also has the ability to obliterate files beyond recovery unless there is a utility running that saves all intermediate versions of files when they are overwritten. You can download the latest version of DELETE from Supernet's FTP server at *ftp://ftp.csn.net/mpj/public/*.

NUKE32S.ZIP (17KB) NUKE v3.2 takes free disk space—space where files may reside that you've deleted—and allocates it to a file called *WIPEDISK.NUK*. The file is then deleted. This removes any useful information that may have still existed in unused disk space. To find the latest version of NUKE, contact its developer Dustin Cook at *gremlin5@juno.com*, or go online and use FILEZ (*www.filez.com*) and search on the file name *nuke32s.zip*.

WIPE-302.ZIP (10KB) Wipe v3.02 is a freeware DOS file shredder developed by Enver J. Berkes. Wipe operates in two modes: Quick Deletion and Full Deletion. The Quick

Deletion doesn't actually overwrite the file, but the file's length will appear as 0. The Full Deletion method overwrites your data. When operated from Windows, Wipe prompts you for input. You can get the latest updates from Wipe's developer Jem Berkes at bP Software (*bpsoft@bigfoot.com*), or you can download the current version from *atc.nethosting.com/starlink/bp/shareware/wipe-302.zip*.

WIPEVK11.ZIP (15.3KB) Wipe v1.1, developed by Vesa Kolhinen of Finland, is a freeware DOS utility that wipes out files by overwriting them. To find the latest version, try contacting V. Kolhinen via his Web page at *www.jyu.fi/~vjko/* or by searching on the file name **wipevk11.zip** (or subsequent file names may be named *wipevk12.zip*, etc.) at sites such as FILEZ at *www.filez.com*.

ZIP.ZAP (148KB) MicroZap is a security program designed for law enforcement and military use for erasing sensitive data stored in computer files. When MicroZap deletes a file, it overwrites the file so that none of the original data remains. First it overwrites the entire file with 0s and then it overwrites the file with 1s. This process repeats itself up to six times. On the final pass, MicroZap writes the hexadecimal value 'F6' in every byte, which is the same thing that format does. To download the latest version, contact New Technologies, Inc. at *ip@secure-data.com*.

Directory Name: MISC
Contents: Miscellaneous Utilities

BURNS100.ZIP (126KB) Mr. Burns is a Windows 3.x security utility that tracks, meters, and monitors what is happening on networked or standalone PCs. Mr. Burns maintains a daily log that lists which applications were run, how long they were run, and how often. You can use Mr. Burns to monitor the use of licensed software to see how popular it is. To find the latest version of this Shareware on the Net, go to ESM Software's Web site at *ourworld.compuserve. com/homepages/esmsoftware/*, or search on the text string **burns100.zip** using FTP Search v3.5 located at *ftpsearch.ntnu.no/ftpsearch*.

GATWY201.ZIP (85KB) GateWAY 2.01, developed by Nickolas Wanke of Adafinn Software, Inc., is a front-end security tool that can support up to 30 different users, each with a different password. GateWAY protects your system during bootup by disabling the F5 and F8 keys and the CTRL+Break during *AUTOEXEC.BAT* bootup. It also locks the keyboard when the computer has been halted. This helps prevent hackers from breaking into the system. GateWAY also logs certain events including when users login, when incorrect attempts to login were tried, guest logins, and when the computer was halted. You can find out what the latest version of GateWAY is by contacting Wanke at *nickw@acay.com.au* or by Wanke's Web site at *www.acay.com.au/~nickw/*.

MICRO_ID.ZIP (223KB) MICRO-ID is used to mark computer hard disks with computer ownership information. This helps police identify ownership when it is recovered as stolen property. MICRO-ID is a product of New Technologies, Inc. For the latest version of MICRO-ID, visit New Technologies' Web site at *http://www.secure-data.com/*.

QP41W31.EXE (305KB) QUICKPICK 4.1 is an electronic tool that helps you calculate system load when determining what size UPS (Uninterruptible Power Supply) to purchase. *QP41W31.EXE* is a self-extracting ZIP File for WIN 3.1 and Windows for Workgroups. QUICKPICK is a trademarked product of MINUTEMAN. You can reach MINUTEMAN at 1–800–238–7272 to inquire if there are updated versions of QUICKPICK available.

QP41W95.EXE (478KB) This version of QUICKPICK 4.1 is a self-extracting ZIP File for WINDOWS 95 and Windows NT.

SCRSAVER.ZIP (71KB) SCRSaver is a Windows 95 freeware application that enables you to startup your screen saver immediately by double-clicking on an icon in the Windows 95 traybar. SCRSaver was developed by Jin Gang of ST Computers, Singapore. To download the latest version, try using FTP search v3.5 in Trondheim, Norway (*ftpsearch.ntnu.no/ftpsearch*) searching on the filename **scrsaver.zip**. If that doesn't work, contact the author at *Jing@stcs.com.sg*.

SURFSPY.ZIP (258KB) The Surfing Spy from ESM Software is a Windows 95 program that logs which Web sites individuals visit while running Internet Explorer or Netscape Navigator. While The Surfing Spy runs hidden in the background, it quietly saves data to a log file. You can learn more about The Surfing Spy and stay up-to-date on the latest version by visiting The Surfing Spy's Web site at *ourworld.compuserve.com/homepages/esmosoftware/spy.htm*.

Directory Name: PSSWRD
Contents: Password Management Utilities

KEEPER.ZIP (620KB) Password Keeper 4.0 helps you keep track of your passwords, registration numbers, and any other information you give it. Brad Harley, the developer of Password Keeper, distributes copies of his software to various download sites. To stay up-to-date with the latest version, try searching on the file name **keeper.zip** using FILEZ at *www.filez.com* or FTP search v3.5 in Trondheim, Norway (*ftpsearch.ntnu.no/ftpsearch*). You might also try looking at *www.ior.com/~bharley/files/keeper.zip*.

PASMEM10.EXE (3,000KB) Password Memorizer for Windows 95 is a shareware program that enables you to store, delete, and modify passwords. For the latest version, visit The Limit Software, Inc. home page at *www.thlimitsoft.com*.

PASSKEEP.ZIP (105KB) Password Keeper v3.2 for Windows 95 is a freeware password utility developed by Gregory Braun from Milwaukee, Wisconsin. Password Keeper enables you to store, edit, and print passwords. Each file you create is encrypted for security and can hold up to 1,000 account entries. To download the latest version of Password Keeper for Windows 95, visit Braun's Software Design Web site at *www.execpc.com/~sbd/*.

PASSP195.ZIP (1,261KB) Passwords Plus 2.1 is a Windows 95 shareware program that allows an unlimited number of individuals to maintain a password-protected l i s t of their passwords. Passwords Plus can generate a random list of passwords and it keeps track of when passwords were last changed. Passwords can be transferred from Password Plus to other applications via Windows clipboard. You can find the latest version of Password Plus on Author Direct Shareware's Web site at *www.dlcwest.com/~sorev/*.

PC.ZIP (1,960KB) David M. Fornalsky is the developer of Password Corral. This password utility is designed to help you organize all of your network and system passwords in one place. DES encryption is used to protect the data you store in files. Visit Cygnus Productions' home page to download the latest version of Password Corral. You can find them on the Web at *www.mcs.com/~cygnus*.

PINMAN.ZIP (135KB) PINMAN is a Windows 95 password management utility developed by Alexander Hummel. The latest zip file is available for download from Hummel's Web site at *www.getsoftware.com/@lexis/pinman/*.

PTRACK.ZIP (901KB) Password Tracker 2.17 helps you manage user names and passwords for programs. Enter the information (user name, password, etc.) into Password Tracker's database, assign the program Window where you want the information to go, and you're done. The next time you need to enter user name and password information, click on the Password Tracker icon in the System Tray, pick the correct data, and it is automatically inserted into the program. To download the latest version, visit Password Tracker's Web site at *www.xnet.com/~robertc/PassTrak.html*.

REVEL11.EXE (1,263KB) SnadBoy's Revelation v1.1 for Windows 95 is a freeware application that remembers passwords, such as the password to access your Internet service provider's dial-up account. Go to SnadBoy Software's Web site at *www.snadboy.com* to download the latest version of Revelation.

SETUPPPV.EXE (965KB) Personal Password Vault (PPV) is a password holding utility for Windows 95 developed by Michael Prince. It stores your passwords and login information in encrypted files using your master password for encryption. Visit PrinceSoft's Web site at *members.aol.com/princesoft/index.htm* to download the latest version of PPV.

THIEF100.ZIP (162KB) The Password Thief for Windows 95 runs in the background recording all passwords that are entered. It catches screen saver passwords, login passwords, or any other password entered in any program. You can use Password Thief to help you keep track of the passwords you forget or to keep others from encrypting files that you need access to. To find the latest version of this shareware on the Net, go to ESM Software's Web site at *ourworld.compuserve.com/homepages/esmsoftware/*, or search on the text string **thief100.zip** using FTP Search v3.5 located at *ftpsearch.ntnu.no/ftpsearch*.

WHISPER.ZIP (418KB) Whisper is a free password management utility developed by Shaun Ivory. Version 1.06 is included on the CD-ROM that accompanies this book. Whisper includes a built-in password generator and it can automatically run backups each time you save your password files. You can contact Shaun Ivory at *shaun@ivory.org* and you get the latest version of his software at *www.ivory.org/free.html*.

WPASSCRK.ZIP (20KB) This is a Word for Windows Password Cracker created by Fauzan Mirza. This program attempts to recover passwords from encrypted Word documents. For details on where to find the latest version available, contact the author at *fauzan@dcs.rhbnc.ac.uk*.

Directory Name: TEXT
Contents: Text Files (MS-WORD)

BOOT.DOC (9KB - Word format) Instructions for creating emergency boot discs for Windows 3.x/DOS platforms.

CHECK.DOC (12KB - Word format) Check-off list to help you recognize potential threats in your PC system.

DATA.DOC (12KB - Word format) Computer equipment information gathering sheet.

POLICY1.TXT (4KB - Plain ASCII text) This is a sample computer security policy that allows you to insert your organization's name.

Index

About the Author

Allen C. Benson is the Director of Library Services at Arkansas State University Mountain Home. He earned his Master of Library Science Degree from the University of Alabama, where he was also awarded the Faculty Scholar Award in 1993. Benson is known for his pioneering work in integrating Internet services into traditional library practices. He is the author of the national bestseller *The Complete Internet Companion for Librarians* (Neal-Schuman Publishers, Inc., 1995), *The Neal-Schuman Complete Internet Companion for Librarians* (Neal-Schuman Publishers, Inc., 1997), and co-author of *Connecting Kids and the Internet* (Neal-Schuman Publishers, Inc., 1996).